PICTURE YOUR PET
IN CROSS STITCH

Claire Crompton

Over 400 animal portraits and motifs

David and Charles

A DAVID & CHARLES BOOK
David & Charles is a subsidiary of F+W (UK) Ltd.,
an F+W Publications Inc. company

First published in the UK in 2005
Designs and text Copyright © Claire Crompton 2005
Photography and layout Copyright © David & Charles 2005

Distributed in North America
by F+W Publications, Inc.
4700 East Galbraith Road
Cincinnati, OH 45236
1-800-289-0963

A catalogue record for this book is available from the British Library.

ISBN 0 7153 2070 X

Executive commissioning editor Cheryl Brown
Editor Jennifer Proverbs
Art editor Prudence Rogers
Designer Louise Prentice
Photographers Karl Adamson and Kim Sayer
Project editor and chart preparation Lin Clements
Production controller Ros Napper

Printed in China by SNP Leefung
for David & Charles
Brunel House   Newton Abbot   Devon

Visit our website at www.davidandcharles.co.uk

David & Charles books are available from all good bookshops; alternatively you can contact our
Orderline on (0)1626 334555 or write to us at FREEPOST EX2110, David & Charles Direct, Newton Abbot
TQ12 4ZZ (No stamp required UK mainland).

CONTENTS

INTRODUCTION

The benefits of owning a pet are countless: a walk is more fun when accompanied by a dog; returning home is more enjoyable when welcomed by a purring cat; stresses are soothed away by watching aquarium fish; caring for a hamster or rabbit teaches a child responsibility – the list is endless. In return for a comfortable home, food and love, your pet gives you unwavering affection, companionship and a lot of fun.

This book is about the joys of pets and more particularly the fun to be had picturing them in cross stitch. The book is packed with hundreds of detailed and realistic charted motifs for all kinds of pets – dogs, cats, rabbits, guinea pigs, hamsters, gerbils, mice, rats, ferrets, birds, fish, reptiles, lizards, horses and even farmyard animals. In the dog and cat chapters there are pages of charted sayings and quotations that will have you nodding in agreement – does your dog or cat walk all over you? There are also many borders and alphabets to allow you to customize the designs and create your own samplers. Throughout the charts, alternate coat colours are given where appropriate so you can personalize a chart to faithfully represent your pet – see overleaf for Choosing Different Coat Colours, which explains how to make these changes.

Apart from masses of charts, each chapter has a selection of attractive projects, giving you lots of ideas on how to use the designs – you will see how easy it is to stitch a calendar of cute puppies, a bookmark with a vivid parrot, a horse portrait in a rosette, a washbag covered in colourful fish and much more. Making up instructions are given for these projects from page 100 onwards and the stitching techniques you will need are explained on pages 98–99.

Whether you are a cat lover, horse mad, canine crazy or a fish fanatic, this book is for you. Use it to create your own unique designs featuring that special someone in your life – your pet.

Welcome Sampler
The chickens and geese shown opposite make a delightful sampler to welcome guests. The designs (charts on page 96) are stitched on cream 14-count Aida using two strands of DMC stranded cotton (floss) for cross stitch and one for backstitch, with 'Welcome' (alphabet on page 65) stitched over two threads of a piece of cream 28-count evenweave. Making up instructions are on page 103. Using some of the many designs in the book you could work this sampler using motifs that reflect your pet passions or use another saying, such as 'Home Sweet Home'.
Stitch count for sampler shown: 89 x 89.
Design size: 18 x 18cm (7 x 7in) on 14-count.

4

Using the Charts

This book is intended to provide an extensive range of charted cross stitch designs for all sorts of pets – large and small, ordinary and exotic. As many breeds have a variety of coat colours, the keys to the charts have been designed to allow you to change the colourway, which means you can personalize a chart to match your pet's coat colour.

In addition, the many pet designs are intended to be used in a multitude of ways, to decorate single items or be combined in large samplers. Three samplers are shown – the Welcome Sampler (previous page), The Love of Dogs sampler overleaf and The Love of Cats sampler (page 45), and on the opposite page you will find suggestions for creating your own samplers.

Choosing Different Coat Colours

The charts in the book are accompanied by a key, indicating which colour of DMC stranded cotton (floss) to use. Symbols have also been used to help further identify some colours. General information on using charts and keys can be found on page 98. Where a breed has a variety of coat colours, the key gives these alternative colour code numbers. Sometimes the nose and eye colour may change too. See the chart and key below as an example of how a chocolate Labrador Retriever can be stitched as the chocolate version or as a black or yellow version.

I have tried to provide all of the colourways on the breed pages by giving alternate colours on different charts. This makes the charts throughout the book highly versatile. For example, for the Persian cats (charted on page 48), one chart has red, black, white and chocolate coat colours, and another chart has blue, cream and lilac coat colours. On three of the charts, the coat has been charted using four shades, ranging through light, medium, dark and very dark. So the walking Persian at the top of the page can also be worked as a blue, cream or lilac cat by referring to the key for the sitting cats at the bottom of the page. The sitting cats could be worked in red, black, white or chocolate by the same method. The coat colours are sometimes abbreviated, e.g. chocolate is called 'choc'. The code numbers refer to DMC threads.

Stitched as a black Labrador Retriever

Stitched as a yellow Labrador Retriever

The chocolate Labrador Retriever

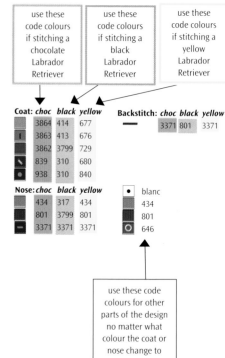

use these code colours if stitching a chocolate Labrador Retriever

use these code colours if stitching a black Labrador Retriever

use these code colours if stitching a yellow Labrador Retriever

Coat:	choc	black	yellow
	3864	414	677
	3863	413	676
	3862	3799	729
	839	310	680
	938	310	840

Backstitch:	choc	black	yellow
—		3371	801	3371

Nose:	choc	black	yellow
	434	317	434
	801	3799	801
	3371	3371	3371

•	blanc
	434
	801
O	646

use these code colours for other parts of the design no matter what colour the coat or nose change to

Black and White Coat Colours

When black or white are given as alternate coat colours, some DMC numbers may appear as alternatives for two colours in the key, i.e. they appear twice in the same key. This is because black and white coats don't have as much shading as other coat colours. So when stitching a black or white coat, keep to the key as it is written.

Stitching Noses and Eyes

Stitch noses and eyes as given in the key, changing the colours as appropriate. Where nose or eye colour is the same across all breed coat colours then just one code will appear in the key. Many of the eyes have a small stitch of white in them: either work this as a quarter cross stitch or as a full cross stitch of eye colour with a small white stitch on top. This speck of white adds a glint to your pet's eye and makes it more lifelike.

Designing a Sampler

You will find creating your own sampler using the many pet motifs, borders, sentiments and alphabets is great fun and even a beginner can design a sampler to feature a collection of favourite pets or animals, either for yourself, your family or for friends.

Using the Motifs

The motifs you choose will depend on personal preference and the reasons why you wish to create a sampler. It might be for a cat fanatic who will be amused to see cats in humorous situations. It might be for a dog lover to display their favourite breeds. It might be for a fish fancier who's just bought an aquarium and longs to show off their colourful tropical fish.

For a cat sampler, you could use cats of one breed or mix breeds together like the sampler shown right. A sampler of puppies (pages 38, 39) would be fun to do or it could have a theme of working dogs using spaniels (pages 16, 17) or sheepdogs (pages 30, 31). How about a cute sampler of rabbits (pages 68, 69) or guinea pigs (page 70) for a child? Whatever your favourite pet, there are plenty of motifs to choose from.

Once you have chosen your motifs, photocopy them or draw the outline on to graph paper. Cut them out and arrange them around other parts of the design such as a saying or with borders, until you have a design that you are happy with.

Adding Text

Many samplers feature a saying or quotation, often a humorous one. You could stitch the one charted or use one of the alphabets given at the end of the dog and cat chapters to chart your own. Instead of a motto, how about adding your pet's name and details about when and where you got them? Chart the words in the centre of a piece of graph paper to check the spacing works correctly before beginning to stitch.

Adding Borders

The three samplers shown in the book use simple borders to add interest and highlight areas of the design and there are plenty of other borders to choose from at the end of the dog and cat chart pages.

Calculating Design Size

Once you have designed your sampler you will need to count the total numbers of stitches across the height and width to work out the design's overall size before you cut your fabric – see calculating design size page 98. If you wish to include a lot of motifs and detail you might find working on a higher count fabric would be best, e.g., a 16-count rather than a 14-count.

Sampler Design Ideas

- If you chose a theme for your sampler you will find it easier to select appropriate motifs.
- Try using a mirror to create a mirror image of a motif, so the pet or decorative motif is facing the opposite way.
- Try repeating a motif to form a border, perhaps working each repeat in a different coat colour. The Siamese cats chasing a butterfly (page 50) or the running guinea pigs (page 70) could be repeated to make a border or a panel in the centre of the sampler. Draw or stick the motifs on to graph paper so they fit together in a pleasing way.

- Make a feature of a saying or motto, placing it at the top, centre or bottom of the sampler and surrounding it with repeated motifs or borders.
- Use the different alphabets to customize your sampler, adding names, dates, events, pet details and so on, planning the words out on graph paper first to ensure they fit.
- Try working a border around the whole design, to tie all the elements together.
- Look at the samplers on pages 5, 9 and 45 to give you more ideas for arranging your motifs and how to space them.

DOGS

This chapter has everything the dog lover needs – dogs, dogs and more dogs! There are loving dogs, handsome dogs and game-for-anything dogs – perfect on gifts for friends and family. There's inspiration overleaf but you will find many more uses for the designs, such as a dog portrait on an album of favourite snapshots, dogs playing on a sewing box lid or a tumble of puppies as a picture for a child's room.

The chapter has a page of charts for each of the 22 most popular breeds, ranging from Boxers to Spaniels, Beagles to Terriers. There are also single motifs for a further 18 breeds, so there is plenty to choose from. Alternative coat colours are given where appropriate so if you don't see your dog it is easy to alter a chart (see Choosing Different Coat Colours page 6). Cross breeds and puppies aren't forgotten – there are lots of fun designs for each. Finally, there are dog-inspired sayings to delight your canine-crazy friends, plus borders, alphabets and motifs to help you customize the designs.

The Dog Rules!

Owner
- Be firm at the dinner table and discourage your dog from begging for scraps.
- Throw sticks when out walking; it's good exercise for your dog who will love retrieving them.
- Don't allow your dog on sofas and beds as this will create bad habits that will be difficult to break.
- Show your dog who is boss and discourage him from barking when the doorbell rings.

Dog
- Beg regularly at the dinner table and your owner will soon learn to leave you scraps.
- Your owner will throw sticks when out walking but it takes a while for them to realize they must also retrieve them – be patient.
- Always sleep on sofas and beds as this will make your owner feel secure, knowing you are there to guard them.
- Bark loudly and keep barking when the doorbell rings as your owner will then get rid of the visitor and have more time for you.

The Love of Dogs Sampler
The sampler opposite shows how some of the wonderful dogs and puppies charted in this chapter can be used. The sentiment, echoed by all dog lovers, is framed by a fun bone border but you could easily change this – see pages 42 and 43 for ideas and alphabets. The sampler is stitched on white 14-count Aida with two strands of stranded cotton (floss) for cross stitch and one for backstitch. To plan your own sampler, see page 7 for ideas.
Stitch count for sampler shown: 139 x 110.
Design size: 25.2 x 20cm (10 x 7¾in) on 14-count.

Grrreat Gifts!

Let's make no bones about it, there are ideas here to suit everyone and every room in the house. The wonderful dog and puppy designs charted in this chapter are very versatile and are easily personalized using the messages and alphabets on pages 40–43. So, paws a while to check out the charts and then get stitching! Refer to the list of suppliers on page 104 for the items used.

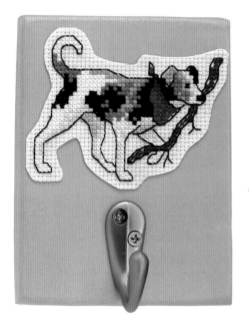

A lead hook is ideal for keeping your dog's lead handy. This dog (page 37), all set for a long muddy ramble, is stitched on 14-count white Aida using two strands of stranded cotton (floss) for cross stitch and one for backstitch. To stop the fabric fraying, back the stitching with heavyweight iron-on interfacing (see page 100). Cut the fabric around the stitching, leaving plenty of fabric around small details. Using PVA glue, stick the design above a coat hook or on to the wooden mount of a ready-mounted hook.

You could make your own hook mount by cutting a piece of wood to size, painting it and screwing on a coat hook. Adding the dog's name will make it even more special. Instead of this motif, why not stitch your own dog or how about a row of hooks for all your dogs?

Stitch count: 34 x 46.
Design size: 6.2 x 8.3cm (2½ x 3¼in) on 14-count.

This fridge magnet with its cute sentiment (page 40) is stitched on 16-count cream Aida using two strands of stranded cotton (floss) for cross stitch and one for backstitch. The design fits into a 4.5 x 7cm (1¾ x 2¾in) fridge magnet. When stitching is completed, cut the fabric to size and put it into the magnet. Cut white paper the same size and put behind the stitching and assemble the magnet according to the manufacturer's instructions.

You could stitch your own dog or a different sentiment but make sure that the motif will fit into the fridge magnet (see calculating design size page 98). Alternatively, you can make your own fridge magnet by sticking the stitched design on to a piece of thick card and gluing a magnet to the back.

Stitch count: 40 x 20.
Design size: 6.3 x 3.2cm (2½ x 1¼in) on 16-count.

A calendar showing a group of adorable puppies (pages 38 and 39) makes a lovely gift for a friend. Stitch on 14-count cream Aida using two strands of stranded cotton (floss) for cross stitch and one for backstitch. When the stitching is completed, mount the design into a ready-made card (see page 101), sticking on a hanging loop and a pocket calendar. You could make your own mount if your design is too big for a card aperture – follow the instructions on page 101.

Instead of the group of puppies, you could stitch a single puppy up to no good – perhaps chewing a shoe (page 38) or shaking the feathers out of a cushion (page 39). Work a different sentiment, such as 'A house is not a home without a dog'.

Stitch count: 53 x 82.
Design size: 9.6 x 14.8cm (3¾ x 5¾in) on 14-count.

A towel border of bounding Irish Wolfhounds (page 32) is great fun and useful too. Stitch on 6.3cm (2½in) wide white 16-count Aida band using two strands of stranded cotton (floss) for cross stitch and one for backstitch. Measure the towel width and cut the band to size, adding 1.5cm (⅝in) at each end for turning under. Mark the centre and place pins to mark the motifs, spacing them evenly along the band. When stitching is completed, pin the band on the towel, turning raw ends under and stitch into place.

Substitute your own dog breed or stitch a mixture of breeds, making sure your chosen design fits on to Aida band, which comes in many widths (see calculating design size page 98). Alternatively, you could stitch a border of dogs on to a piece of Aida fabric, turning under all four raw edges before stitching it on to a towel or tea towel.

Stitch count: each motif 26 x 48.
Design size: 4.2 x 7.6cm (1½ x 3in) on 16-count.

A dog portrait like this deserves to take pride of place amongst the family portraits. This Labrador Retriever (page 12) and her name tag are stitched on 14-count white Aida using two strands of stranded cotton (floss) for cross stitch and one for backstitch. When stitching is completed, mount into a ready-made frame (see page 102). To make the name tag, use the bone chart on page 43 and the backstitch alphabet on page 42. Using graph paper, chart your dog's name and then draw the bone shape around it – you may have to lengthen or shorten the design so the name fits. Stitch the design. To stop the fabric fraying, back the stitching with heavyweight iron-on interfacing (see page 100). Cut around the bone shape, leaving a gap of three squares all around. Stick on to the frame using PVA glue.

Work a portrait of your own dog – one this size would also be wonderful mounted on the front of a journal cover or album, perhaps containing details of your pet or favourite photographs.

Stitch count: dog 47 x 45; name tag 9 x 23.
Design size: dog 8.5 x 8.2cm (3⅜ x 3¼in); name tag 1.6 x 4cm (½ x 1½in) on 14-count.

A drawstring bag is perfect for keeping Duke's (page 13) toys tidy. The patch is stitched on 14-count white Aida using two strands of stranded cotton (floss) for cross stitch and one for backstitch. When stitching is completed, cut the patch into a square with the motif in the centre. Back the patch with heavyweight iron-on interfacing (see page 100) – this will prevent a dark or heavily patterned fabric showing through. Turn under the raw edges and tack (baste) down, then either machine or hand stitch the patch on to a ready-made bag or make your own bag – see page 101 for full instructions. The finished bag size is approximately 35.5 x 40.5cm (14 x 16in).

Stitch your own dog on to an Aida patch and add their name using the alphabets on pages 42 and 43. You could stitch a second smaller bag to keep grooming tools handy.

Stitch count: 42 x 48.
Design size: 7.6 x 8.7cm (3 x 3½in) on 14-count.

A friendly and intelligent family dog, the Labrador Retriever loves long walks and retrieving from water.

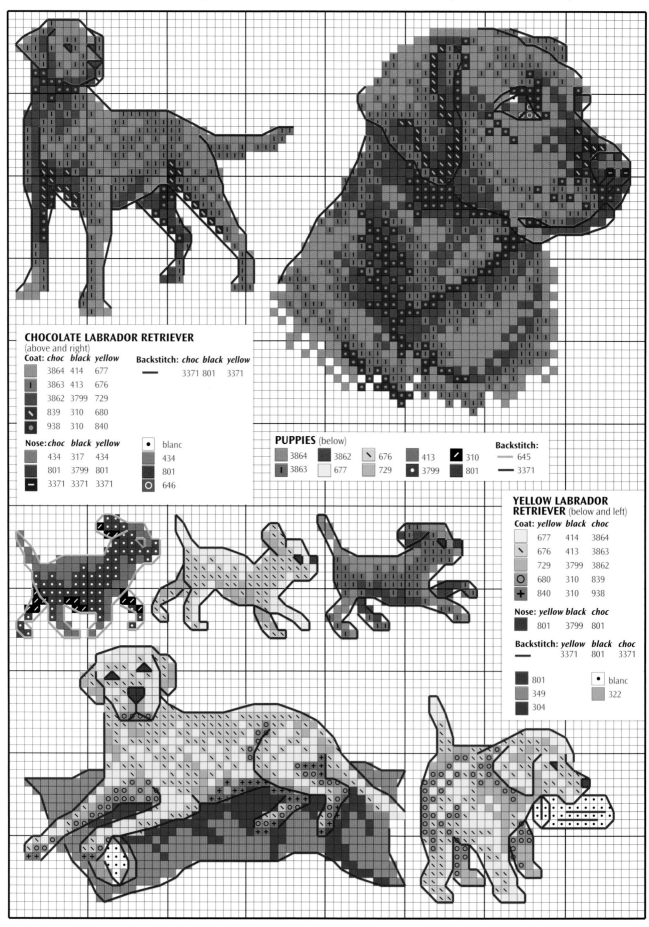

CHOCOLATE LABRADOR RETRIEVER
(above and right)

Coat: *choc* *black* *yellow*

	choc	*black*	*yellow*
	3864	414	677
I	3863	413	676
	3862	3799	729
\	839	310	680
●	938	310	840

Backstitch: *choc* *black* *yellow*

	choc	*black*	*yellow*
—	3371	801	3371

Nose: *choc* *black* *yellow*

	choc	*black*	*yellow*
	434	317	434
	801	3799	801
—	3371	3371	3371

•	blanc
	434
	801
O	646

PUPPIES (below)

	3864		3862	\	676		413	/	310
I	3863		677		729	●	3799		801

Backstitch:
— 645
— 3371

YELLOW LABRADOR RETRIEVER (below and left)

Coat: *yellow* *black* *choc*

	yellow	*black*	*choc*
	677	414	3864
\	676	413	3863
	729	3799	3862
O	680	310	839
+	840	310	938

Nose: *yellow* *black* *choc*

	yellow	*black*	*choc*
	801	3799	801

Backstitch: *yellow* *black* *choc*

	yellow	*black*	*choc*
—	3371	801	3371

	801	•	blanc
	349		322
	304		

The German Shepherd is used as a guard dog and police dog in search and rescue, but is also a loyal companion.

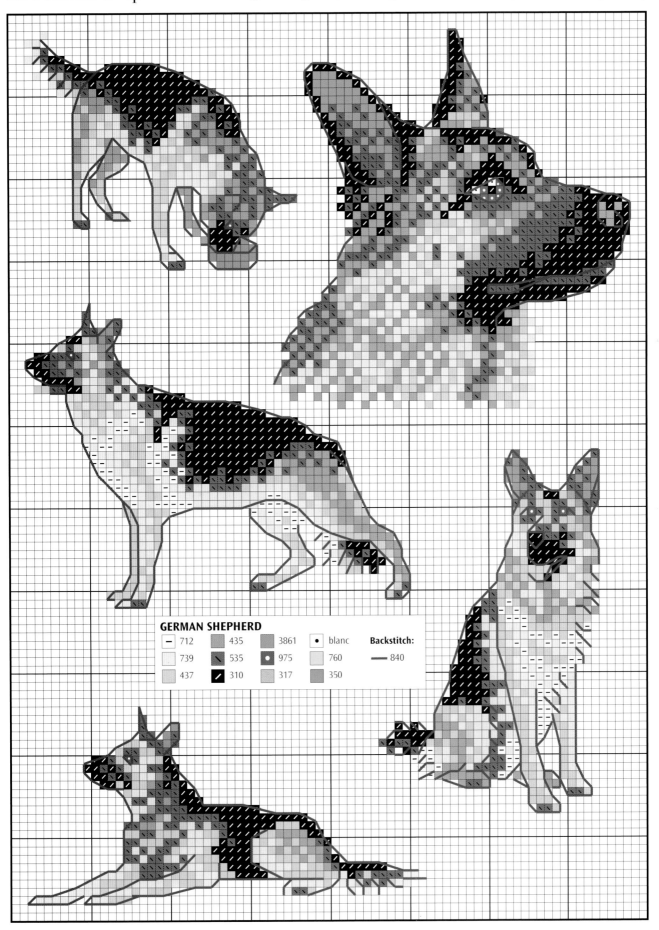

GERMAN SHEPHERD

− 712	435	3861	• blanc	**Backstitch:**
739	535	◉ 975	760	—— 840
437	✦ 310	317	350

With its retrieving abilities and love of water, the Golden Retriever is easy to train but less easy to keep clean!

GOLDEN RETRIEVER

								Backstitch:
—	712	╱	435	• blanc	▨	3031		—— 3371
	738		434			317		3713
	437	⊟	838	◢ 310		931		

The Beagle is naturally exuberant with great stamina and determination, so walks often turn into runs.

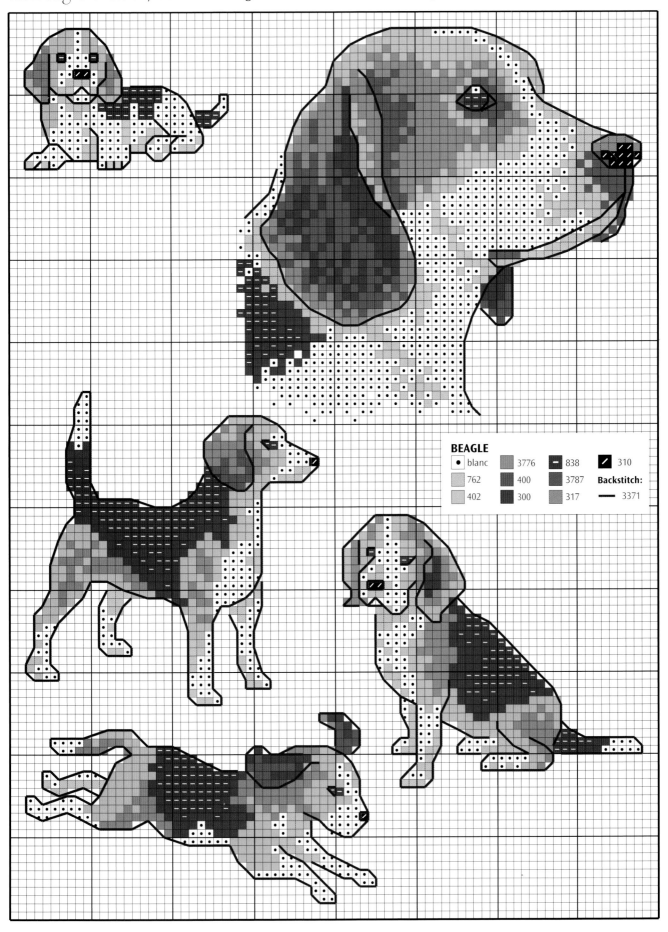

BEAGLE

• blanc	3776	— 838	▨ 310
762	400	3787	**Backstitch:**
402	300	317	— 3371

English Cocker and Spring Spaniels are always searching, always 'springing' – game or people!

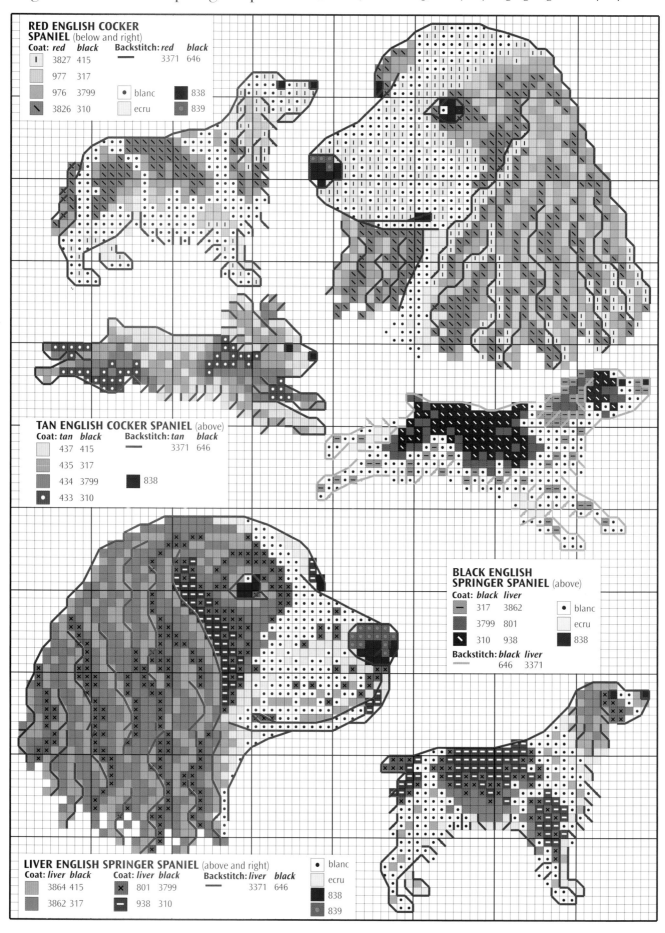

RED ENGLISH COCKER SPANIEL (below and right)

Coat:	*red*	*black*	Backstitch:	*red*	*black*
I	3827	415	—	3371	646
	977	317			
	976	3799	• blanc		838
╲	3826	310	ecru		839

TAN ENGLISH COCKER SPANIEL (above)

Coat:	*tan*	*black*	Backstitch:	*tan*	*black*
	437	415	—	3371	646
	435	317			
	434	3799		838	
⊙	433	310			

BLACK ENGLISH SPRINGER SPANIEL (above)

Coat:	*black*	*liver*		
—	317	3862	•	blanc
	3799	801		ecru
╲	310	938		838
Backstitch:	*black*	*liver*		
	646	3371		

LIVER ENGLISH SPRINGER SPANIEL (above and right)

Coat:	*liver*	*black*	Coat:	*liver*	*black*	Backstitch:	*liver*	*black*
	3864	415	✕	801	3799	—	3371	646
	3862	317	▬	938	310			

•	blanc
	ecru
	838
⊙	839

The Cavalier King Charles and King Charles Spaniels have placid and gentle temperaments.

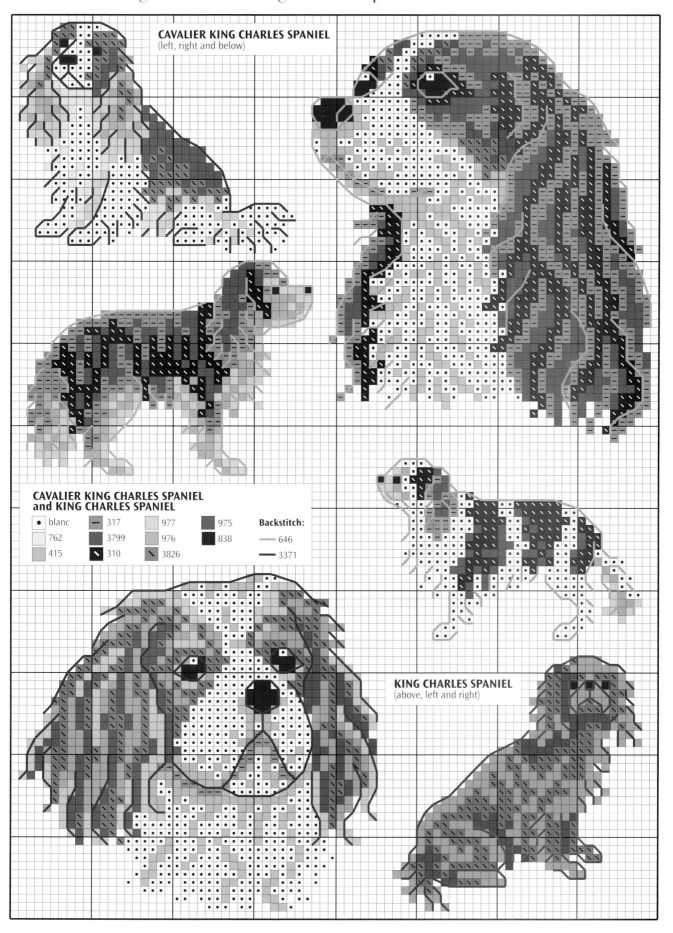

CAVALIER KING CHARLES SPANIEL
(left, right and below)

CAVALIER KING CHARLES SPANIEL
and KING CHARLES SPANIEL

• blanc	— 317	977	975
762	3799	976	838
415	310	3826	

Backstitch:
— 646
— 3371

KING CHARLES SPANIEL
(above, left and right)

Originally bred for hunting, the Dachshund is an affectionate companion – small in stature but big in character.

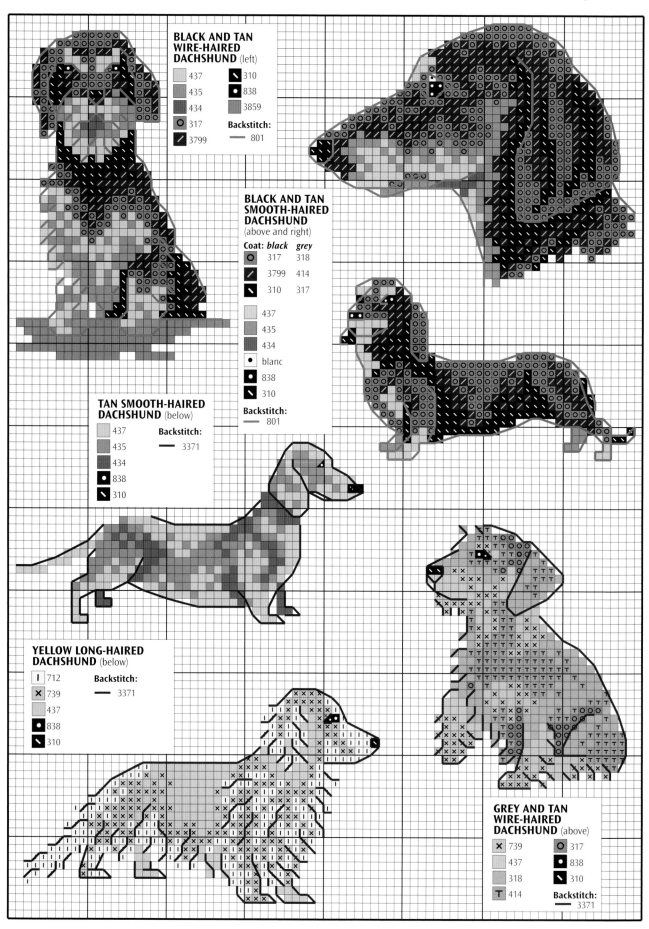

BLACK AND TAN WIRE-HAIRED DACHSHUND (left)

	437	✦	310
	435	•	838
	434		3859
◉	317		
✦	3799		

Backstitch:
— 801

BLACK AND TAN SMOOTH-HAIRED DACHSHUND (above and right)

Coat: *black* *grey*

		black	*grey*
◉		317	318
✦		3799	414
✦		310	317
		437	
		435	
		434	
•		blanc	
•		838	
✦		310	

Backstitch:
— 801

TAN SMOOTH-HAIRED DACHSHUND (below)

		Backstitch:
	437	— 3371
	435	
	434	
•	838	
✦	310	

YELLOW LONG-HAIRED DACHSHUND (below)

		Backstitch:
I	712	— 3371
✕	739	
	437	
•	838	
✦	310	

GREY AND TAN WIRE-HAIRED DACHSHUND (above)

✕	739	◉	317
	437	•	838
	318	✦	310
T	414		

Backstitch:
— 3371

18 DOGS

With an intelligent and proud bearing, the Poodle is the socialite of the canine world.

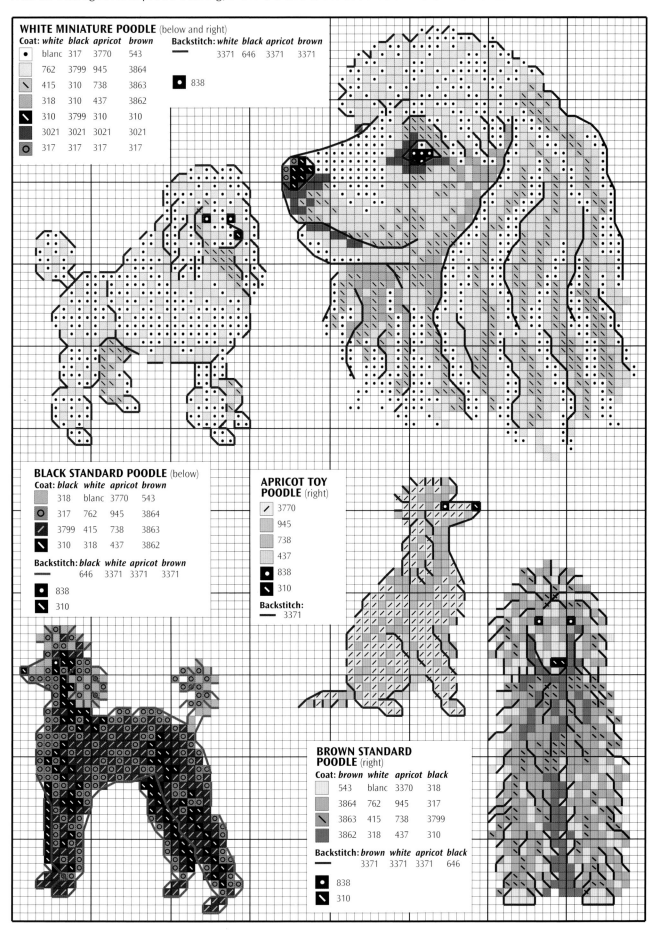

WHITE MINIATURE POODLE (below and right)

Coat:	white	black	apricot	brown	Backstitch:	white	black	apricot	brown
•	blanc	317	3770	543	—		3371	646	3371	3371
	762	3799	945	3864	•	838			
\	415	310	738	3863					
	318	310	437	3862					
\	310	3799	310	310					
	3021	3021	3021	3021					
O	317	317	317	317					

BLACK STANDARD POODLE (below)

Coat:	black	white	apricot	brown
	318	blanc	3770	543
O	317	762	945	3864
/	3799	415	738	3863
\	310	318	437	3862

Backstitch: black white apricot brown

—		646	3371	3371	3371
•	838				
■	310				

APRICOT TOY POODLE (right)

/	3770
	945
	738
	437
•	838
\	310

Backstitch:
— 3371

BROWN STANDARD POODLE (right)

Coat:	brown	white	apricot	black
	543	blanc	3370	318
	3864	762	945	317
\	3863	415	738	3799
	3862	318	437	310

Backstitch: brown white apricot black

—		3371	3371	3371	646
•	838				
■	310				

The Yorkshire Terrier is a true Yorkshire tyke – eager to play but ready to fight.

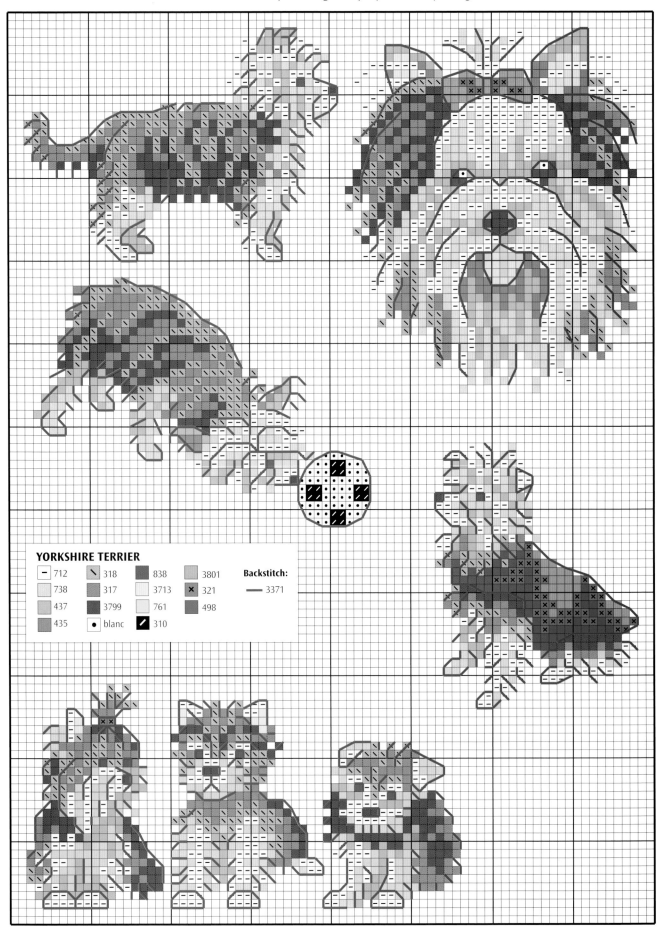

YORKSHIRE TERRIER

− 712	⟍ 318	838	3801	**Backstitch:**
738	317	3713	✕ 321	— 3371
437	3799	761	498	
435	• blanc	◪ 310		

The West Highland White Terrier has a merry expression and eyes full of mischief.

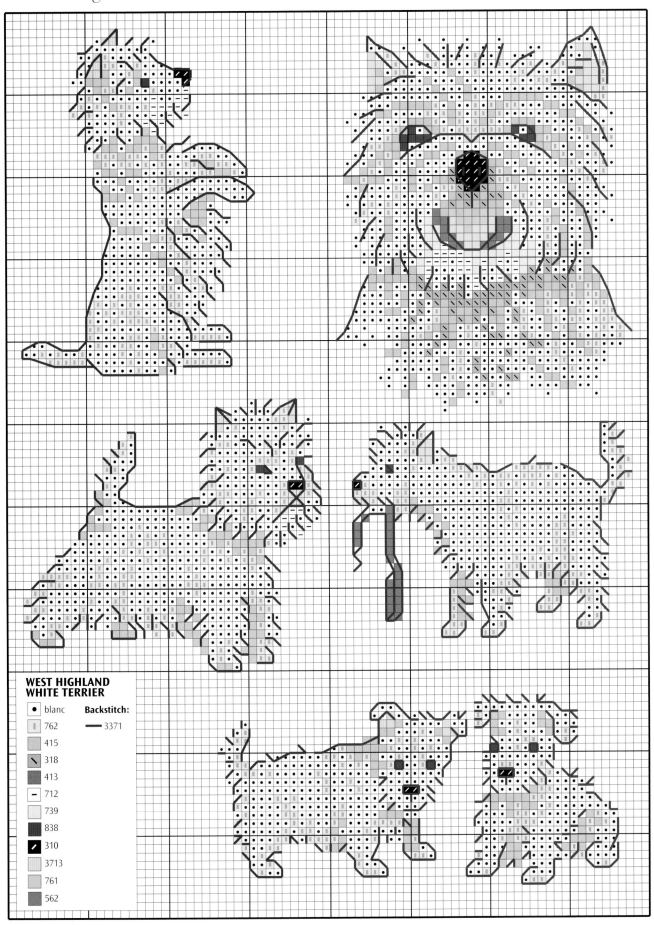

**WEST HIGHLAND
WHITE TERRIER**

•	blanc	**Backstitch:**	
▯	762	— 3371	
▨	415		
◥	318		
▨	413		
−	712		
▨	739		
▨	838		
◿	310		
▨	3713		
▨	761		
▨	562		

A true extrovert, the Boxer will never grow up, always living life at double-quick speed.

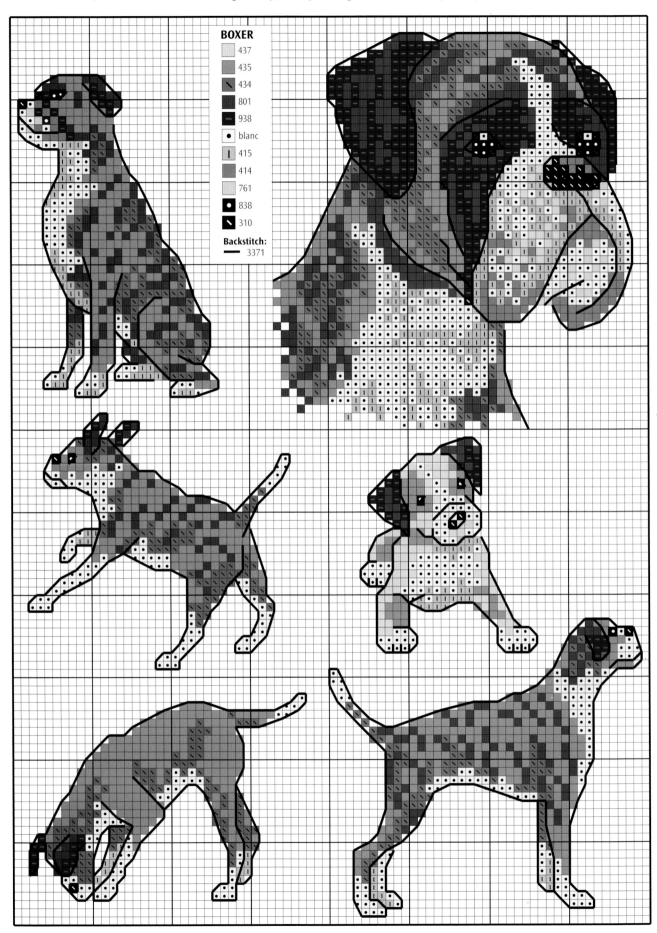

BOXER
- 437
- 435
- 434
- 801
- 938
- • blanc
- | 415
- 414
- 761
- ◉ 838
- 310

Backstitch:
— 3371

The English Bulldog is a symbol of British tenacity: powerfully built, he is friendly but stubborn.

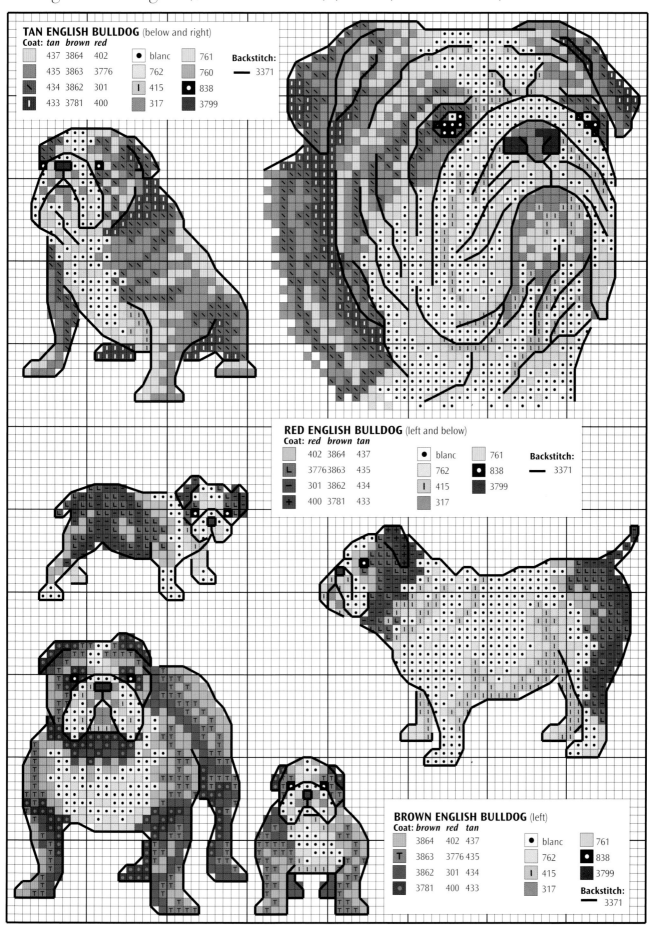

TAN ENGLISH BULLDOG (below and right)
Coat: *tan brown red*

	437	3864	402
	435	3863	3776
	434	3862	301
	433	3781	400

•	blanc	
	762	
I	415	
	317	

	761
	760
◉	838
	3799

Backstitch:
— 3371

RED ENGLISH BULLDOG (left and below)
Coat: *red brown tan*

	402	3864	437
L	3776	3863	435
-	301	3862	434
+	400	3781	433

•	blanc	
	762	
I	415	
	317	

	761
◉	838
	3799

Backstitch:
— 3371

BROWN ENGLISH BULLDOG (left)
Coat: *brown red tan*

	3864	402	437
T	3863	3776	435
	3862	301	434
	3781	400	433

•	blanc
	762
I	415
	317

	761
◉	838
	3799

Backstitch:
— 3371

The Shih Tzu, the Lhasa Lion dog, has a chrysanthemum-like face and a thick coat if left unclipped.

GREY SHIH TZU (above and right)

Coat:	grey	black	brown		Backstitch:	grey	black	brown
●	blanc	blanc	blanc		──	646	646	3371
	762	762	543					
	318	317	3864		I	712		838
	317	3799	3862			738		792
	3799	310	3031			436		

TAN SHIH TZU (above and right)

Coat:	tan	brown	black	white			
I	712	543	318	blanc		●	838
	738	3864	317	762			761
	436	3862	3799	318			792
	435	3031	310	317			

Backstitch:	tan	brown	black	white
──		3371	3371	646	3371

BROWN SHIH TZU
(left and right)

Coat:	brown	black
●	blanc	blanc
	762	762
I	712	318
	738	317
	3864	317
	3862	3799
	3031	310

Backstitch:	brown	black
──		3371	646

● 838

Known as the miniature fox, the Pomeranian is a natural show off, pirouetting and dancing on its lead.

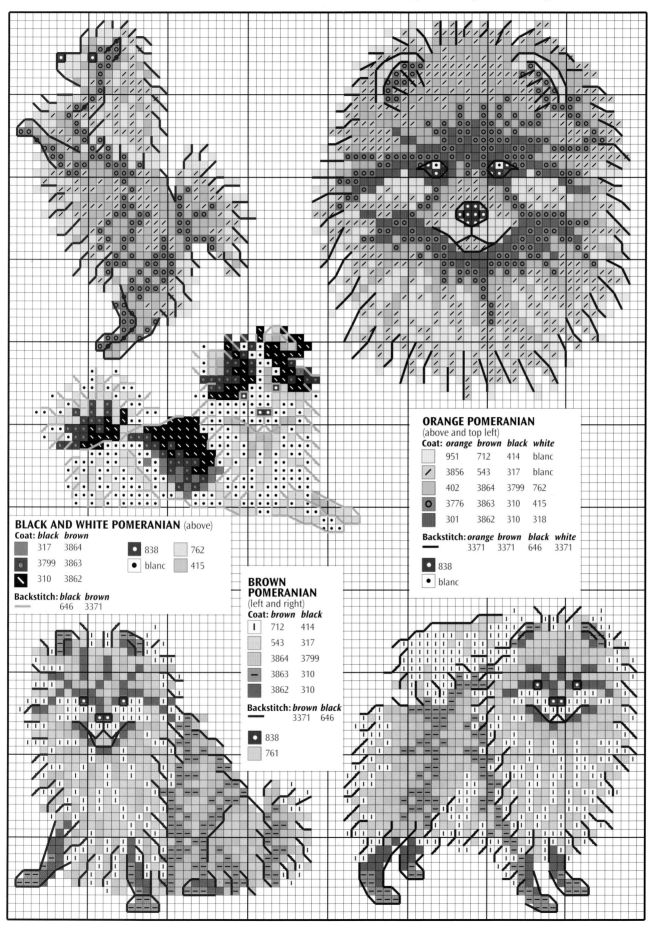

ORANGE POMERANIAN
(above and top left)

Coat:	orange	brown	black	white
	951	712	414	blanc
/	3856	543	317	blanc
	402	3864	3799	762
O	3776	3863	310	415
	301	3862	310	318

Backstitch:	orange	brown	black	white
—		3371	3371	646	3371

	838	
•	blanc	

BLACK AND WHITE POMERANIAN (above)

Coat:	black	brown
	317	3864
	3799	3863
	310	3862

	838			762
•	blanc			415

Backstitch:	black	brown
—	646	3371

BROWN POMERANIAN
(left and right)

Coat:	brown	black
I	712	414
	543	317
	3864	3799
–	3863	310
	3862	310

Backstitch:	brown	black
—	3371	646

	838	
	761	

The **Chihuahua** is a brave little dog, always ready to stand up to larger, more aggressive dogs.

FAWN AND WHITE LONG- AND SMOOTH-HAIRED CHIHUAHUA
(left, above left and right)

	712		317
—	738	◉	3799
	437	◉	838
	435		761
•	blanc		**Backstitch:**
	762	—	3371

BLACK AND TAN CHIHUAHUA
(right and below right)

	712
—	738
	317
◉	3799
◨	310
◉	838
	761
	164
	988
Backstitch:	
—	801

WHITE LONG-HAIRED CHIHUAHUA (left)

•	blanc		761
	762		794
	437		793
	435	×	3863
◉	838	◎	3862
◉	3799		**Backstitch:**
		—	3371

The Miniature Schnauzer has a face full of character with luxurious eyebrows and whiskers.

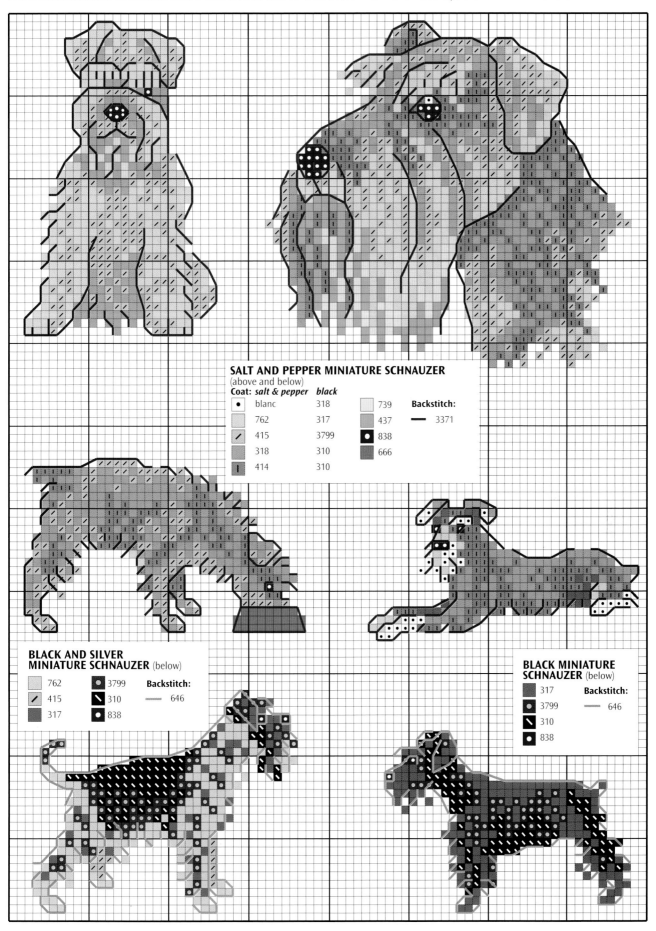

SALT AND PEPPER MINIATURE SCHNAUZER
(above and below)

Coat:	salt & pepper	black				Backstitch:
●	blanc	318			739	— 3371
	762	317			437	
✓	415	3799		●	838	
	318	310			666	
∣	414	310				

**BLACK AND SILVER
MINIATURE SCHNAUZER** (below)

	762	●	3799	Backstitch:
✓	415	✕	310	— 646
	317	●	838	

**BLACK MINIATURE
SCHNAUZER** (below)

	317	Backstitch:
●	3799	— 646
✕	310	
●	838	

The **Rottweiler** is a dog for the experienced owner; good control is rewarded by this strong, courageous guard dog.

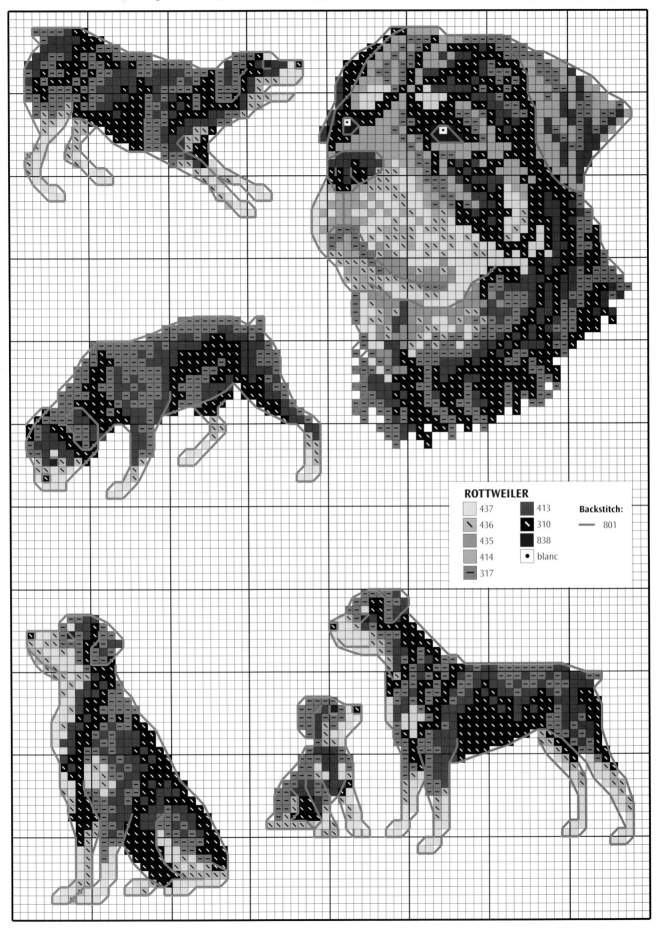

ROTTWEILER

437		413	**Backstitch:**	
436		310	801	
435		838		
414		blanc		
317				

Tough, intelligent and fast moving, the Dobermann is the ultimate guard dog.

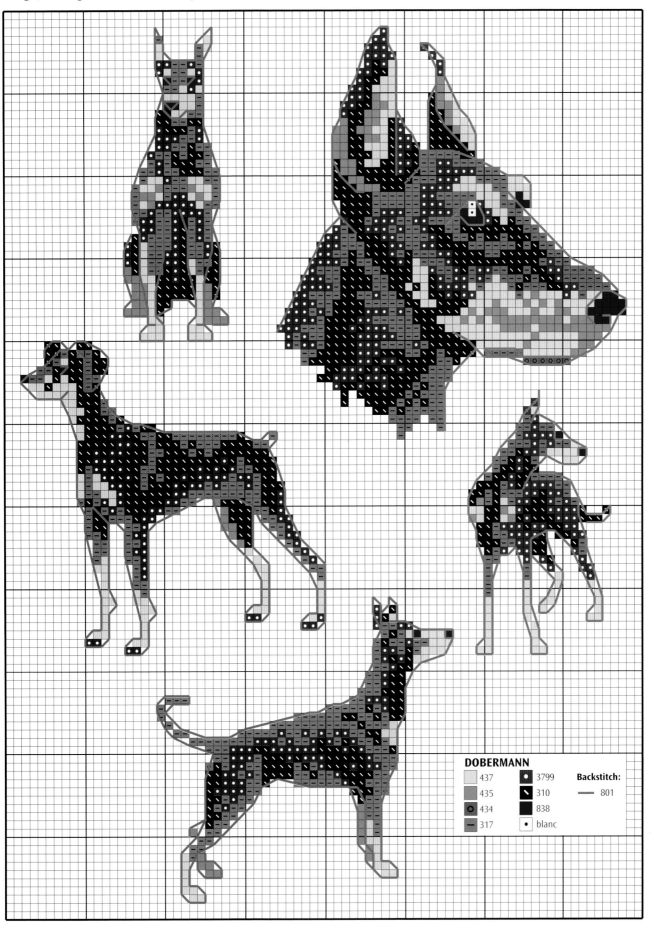

DOBERMANN

437		3799	**Backstitch:**
435		310	801
434		838	
317		blanc	

The Shetland Sheepdog or 'sheltie' has natural herding instincts, making him the organizer in the family.

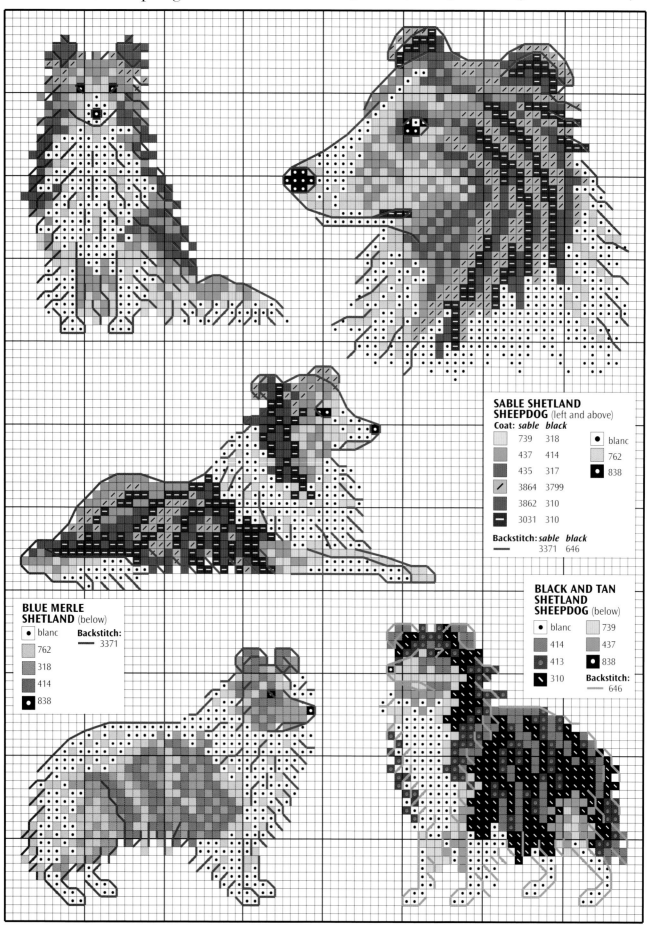

SABLE SHETLAND SHEEPDOG (left and above)
Coat: *sable black*

	sable	*black*		
	739	318	•	blanc
	437	414		762
	435	317	◨	838
/	3864	3799		
	3862	310		
▬	3031	310		

Backstitch: *sable black*
— 3371 646

BLACK AND TAN SHETLAND SHEEPDOG (below)

•	blanc		739
	414		437
◉	413	◨	838
◪	310	**Backstitch:**
		—	646

BLUE MERLE SHETLAND (below)

•	blanc	**Backstitch:**
	762	— 3371
	318	
	414	
◨	838	

30 DOGS

The Border Collie is a classic farm dog, intelligent with herding instincts but can get into mischief if not kept busy.

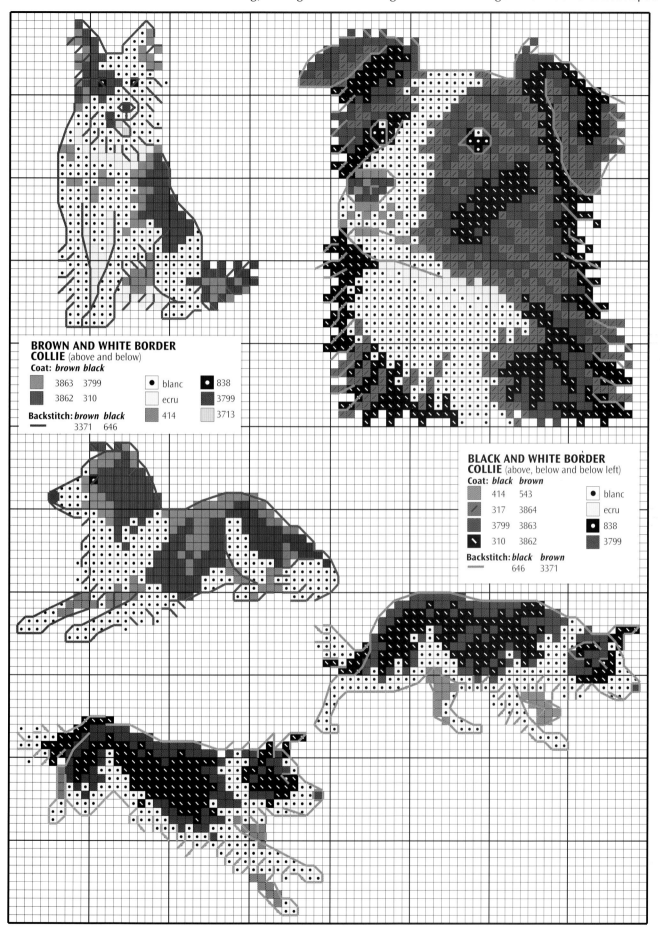

BROWN AND WHITE BORDER COLLIE (above and below)
Coat: *brown black*

▨ 3863	3799	● blanc	◉ 838
▨ 3862	310	▢ ecru	▨ 3799

Backstitch: *brown black*
— 3371 646
▨ 414 ▨ 3713

BLACK AND WHITE BORDER COLLIE (above, below and below left)
Coat: *black brown*

▨ 414	543	● blanc
◪ 317	3864	▢ ecru
▨ 3799	3863	◉ 838
◣ 310	3862	▨ 3799

Backstitch: *black brown*
— 646 3371

Utility Dogs are the workers of the canine world, with hunting, herding and tracking instincts.

GREYHOUND (left)

Coat:	*red*	*white*	*blue*
	3827	blanc	926
	977	762	3768
	3826	415	924

⊙	838	
✕	3799	

Backstitch:
— 3371

ENGLISH SETTER (left)

Coat:	*black*	*liver*
—	3865	3865
	415	3064
	414	3772
◨	310	632

⊙	838

Backstitch:
— 3371

OLD ENGLISH SHEEPDOG (below)

•	blanc		739	**Backstitch:**
	762		437	— 3371
	414	⊙	838	
C	413		761	
✕	3799			

BASSET HOUND (below)

Coat:	*black/tan*	*tan*		
	437	738	•	blanc
	435	437		762
	433	435	⊙	838
◨	310	433		

Backstitch:
— 3371

IRISH WOLFHOUND (right)

Coat:		
	415	**Backstitch:**
	414	— 3371
—	317	
⊙	838	
✕	3799	

Elegant and lithe in build, Hounds have the character and strength of their wild ancestors.

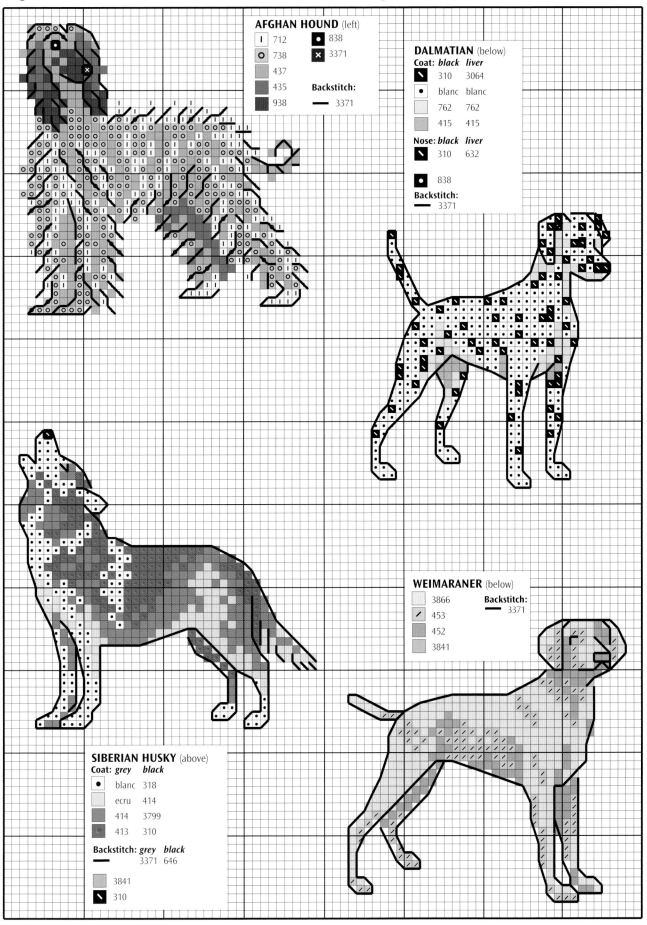

AFGHAN HOUND (left)

I	712	▣	838
○	738	✕	3371
	437		
	435	**Backstitch:**	
	938	—	3371

DALMATIAN (below)

Coat: *black* *liver*

◣	310	3064
•	blanc	blanc
	762	762
	415	415

Nose: *black* *liver*

◣	310	632

▣	838

Backstitch:
— 3371

WEIMARANER (below)

	3866
⁄	453
	452
	3841

Backstitch:
— 3371

SIBERIAN HUSKY (above)

Coat: *grey* *black*

•	blanc	318
	ecru	414
	414	3799
•	413	310

Backstitch: *grey* *black*

—		3371	646

	3841
◣	310

Small in stature but big in elegance and character, Toy Dogs are definitely not lap dogs.

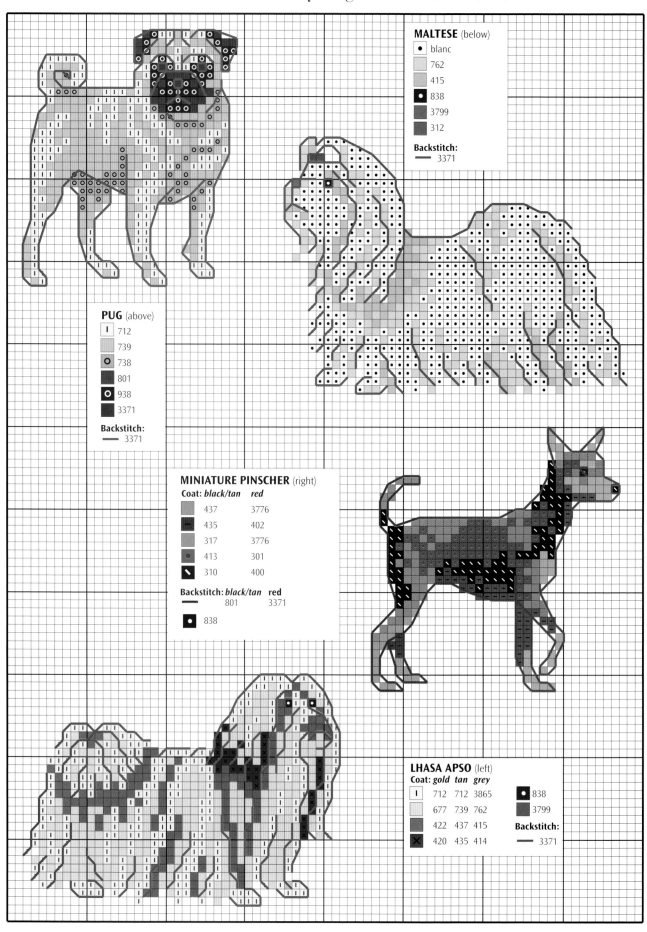

MALTESE (below)
- • blanc
- 762
- 415
- 838
- 3799
- 312

Backstitch:
— 3371

PUG (above)
- I 712
- 739
- ○ 738
- 801
- ◉ 938
- 3371

Backstitch:
— 3371

MINIATURE PINSCHER (right)

Coat:	black/tan	red
	437	3776
	435	402
	317	3776
	413	301
	310	400

Backstitch: black/tan red
— 801 3371

☒ 838

LHASA APSO (left)

Coat:	gold	tan	grey		
I	712	712	3865	☒	838
	677	739	762		3799
	422	437	415	**Backstitch:**
✗	420	435	414	— 3371

Bustling, busy and full of mischief, Terriers are as happy to play as they are to work.

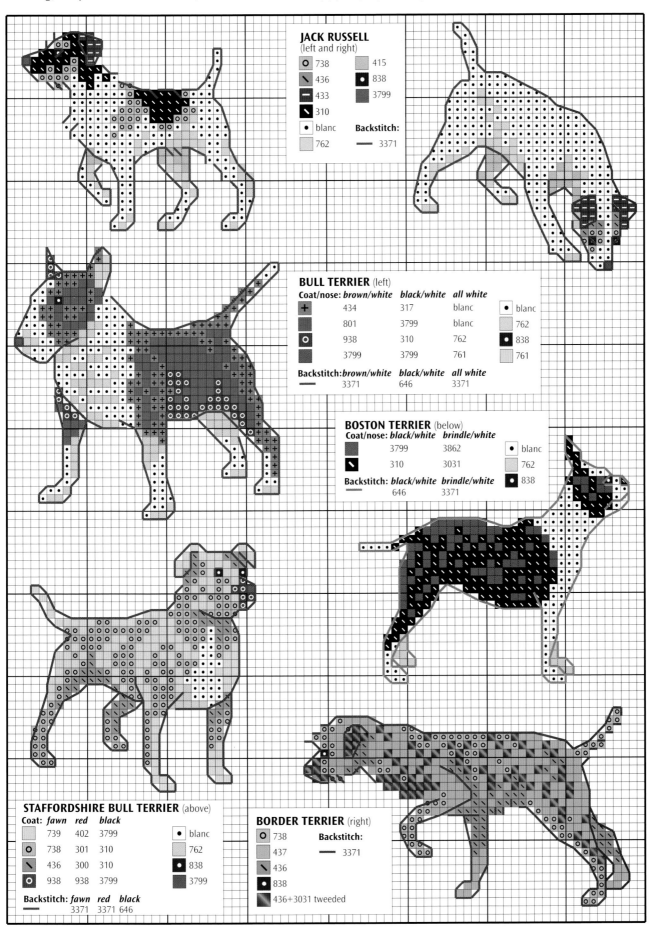

JACK RUSSELL
(left and right)

O	738		415
\	436	◉	838
—	433		3799
\	310		
•	blanc	**Backstitch:**	
	762	—	3371

BULL TERRIER (left)

Coat/nose:	*brown/white*	*black/white*	*all white*		
+	434	317	blanc	•	blanc
	801	3799	blanc		762
◉	938	310	762	◉	838
	3799	3799	761		761
Backstitch:	*brown/white*	*black/white*	*all white*		
—	3371	646	3371		

BOSTON TERRIER (below)

Coat/nose:	*black/white*	*brindle/white*		
	3799	3862	•	blanc
\	310	3031		762
Backstitch:	*black/white*	*brindle/white*	◉	838
—	646	3371		

STAFFORDSHIRE BULL TERRIER (above)

Coat:	*fawn*	*red*	*black*		
	739	402	3799	•	blanc
O	738	301	310		762
\	436	300	310	◉	838
◉	938	938	3799		3799
Backstitch:	*fawn*	*red*	*black*		
—	3371	3371	646		

BORDER TERRIER (right)

O	738	**Backstitch:**	
	437	—	3371
\	436		
■	838		
\	436+3031 tweeded		

Call cross breeds mongrels, mutts, or pooches, a pedigree isn't required for this loving member of the family.

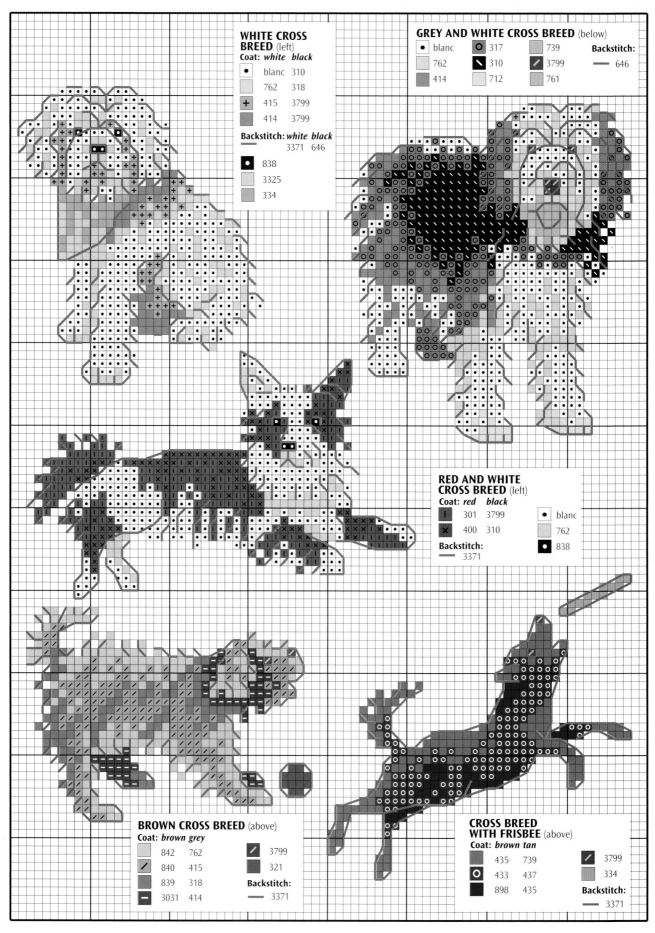

WHITE CROSS BREED (left)
Coat: *white black*

•	blanc	310
	762	318
+	415	3799
	414	3799

Backstitch: *white black*
—	3371	646
◉	838	
	3325	
	334	

GREY AND WHITE CROSS BREED (below)

•	blanc	◉	317		739
	762	◣	310		3799
	414		712		761

Backstitch:
— 646

RED AND WHITE CROSS BREED (left)
Coat: *red black*

▌	301	3799		•	blanc
✕	400	310			762

Backstitch:
—	3371	
◉	838	

BROWN CROSS BREED (above)
Coat: *brown grey*

	842	762		╱	3799
╱	840	415			321
	839	318			
▬	3031	414			

Backstitch:
— 3371

CROSS BREED WITH FRISBEE (above)
Coat: *brown tan*

	435	739		╱	3799
◉	433	437			334
■	898	435			

Backstitch:
— 3371

Mixed ancestors means that each cross breed is **unique**; there isn't another dog like yours in the world.

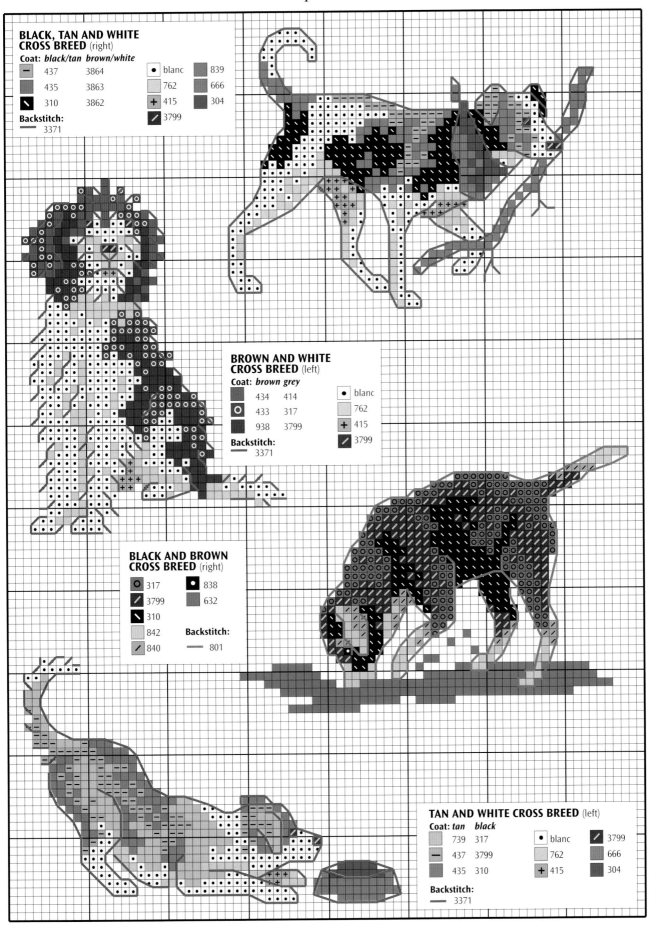

BLACK, TAN AND WHITE CROSS BREED (right)

Coat: *black/tan* *brown/white*

−	437	3864	•	blanc	▨ 839
▨	435	3863		762	▨ 666
◪	310	3862	+	415	▨ 304

Backstitch:
— 3371

⟋ 3799

BROWN AND WHITE CROSS BREED (left)

Coat: *brown grey*

▨	434	414	•	blanc
⊙	433	317		762
▨	938	3799	+	415

Backstitch:
— 3371

⟋ 3799

BLACK AND BROWN CROSS BREED (right)

⊙	317	▨	838
⟋	3799	▨	632
◪	310		
	842	**Backstitch:**	
⟋	840	—	801

TAN AND WHITE CROSS BREED (left)

Coat: *tan* *black*

	739	317	•	blanc	⟋ 3799
−	437	3799		762	▨ 666
▨	435	310	+	415	▨ 304

Backstitch:
— 3371

Training puppies is never easy with their mischievous natures and instinctive curiosity.

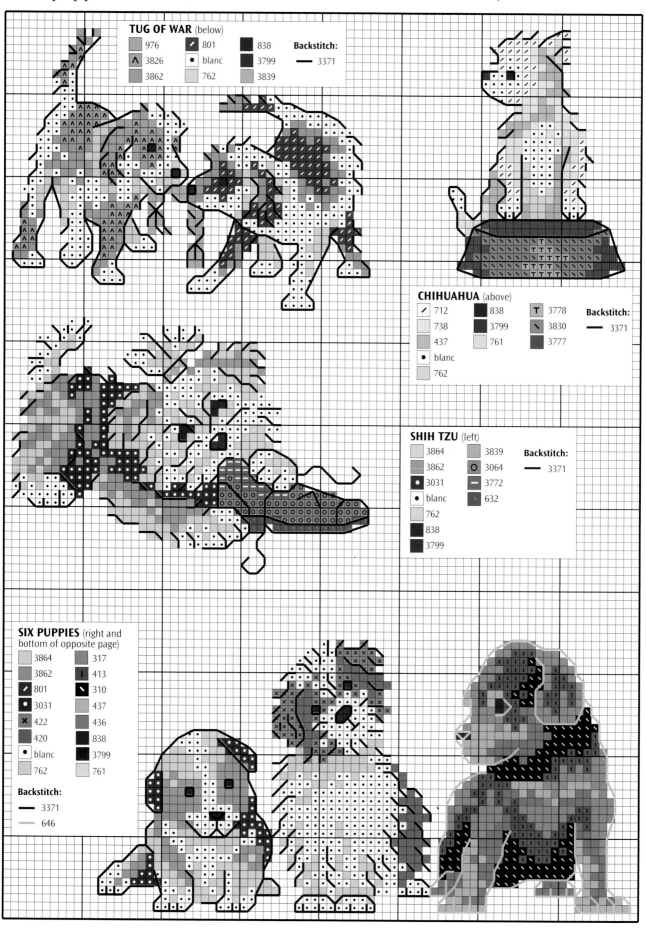

TUG OF WAR (below)

▦ 976	◪ 801	■ 838	**Backstitch:**
⋀ 3826	• blanc	▨ 3799	— 3371
▦ 3862	▦ 762	▦ 3839	

CHIHUAHUA (above)

◢ 712	■ 838	T 3778	**Backstitch:**
▦ 738	▨ 3799	◩ 3830	— 3371
▦ 437	▦ 761	▦ 3777	
• blanc			
▦ 762			

SHIH TZU (left)

▦ 3864	▦ 3839	**Backstitch:**
▦ 3862	◎ 3064	— 3371
◩ 3031	═ 3772	
• blanc	▨ 632	
▦ 762		
■ 838		
▨ 3799		

SIX PUPPIES (right and bottom of opposite page)

▦ 3864	▦ 317
▦ 3862	▮ 413
◪ 801	◣ 310
◩ 3031	▦ 437
✕ 422	▦ 436
▦ 420	■ 838
• blanc	▨ 3799
▦ 762	▦ 761

Backstitch:

— 3371

— 646

38 DOGS

Chewed shoes, puddles on carpets, paw prints on chairs? All is forgiven with one look from those puppy dog eyes!

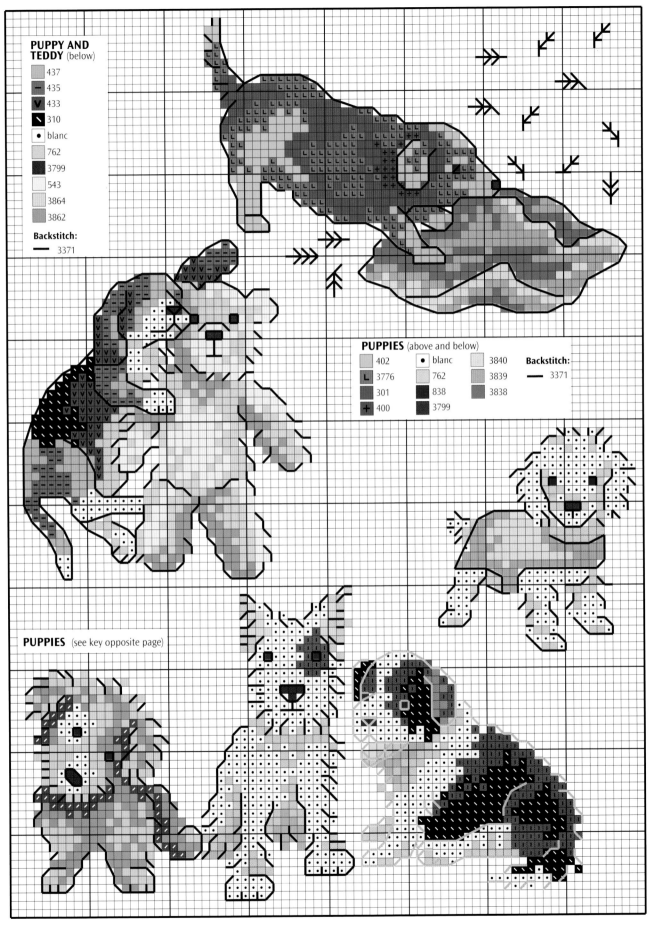

PUPPY AND TEDDY (below)

	437
—	435
V	433
◣	310
•	blanc
	762
	3799
	543
	3864
	3862

Backstitch:

— 3371

PUPPIES (above and below)

								Backstitch:
	402	•	blanc		3840			— 3371
L	3776		762		3839			
	301		838		3838			
+	400		3799					

PUPPIES (see key opposite page)

when 'Please' doesn't work...

Beg!

If you want the best seat in the house...

Friends Fur-ever MOVE THE DOG!

beware of the puppy

It's another bad hair day

Bring your cross stitch pet designs to life with these humorous sayings and fun motifs.

fetch ✗ heel ✗
roll over ✗
beg ✗ speak ✗
lie down ✓

Recycle bones here

Dogs leave
pawprints

on your   heart

Dogs smile
with their tails

N-S

Home Sweet Home

SENTIMENTS

3827	⃝ 437	703	**Backstitch:**
977	435	701	— 3371
976	543	208	— 3826
⊟ 3826	╱ 3864	╲ 758	
• blanc	3863	＋ 3778	**French knots:**
762	840	794	● 3371
414	▮ 838	793	
◣ 310	761	368	
⊟ 453	3733	△ 320	
739	367		

These alphabets can be used to personalize gifts and cards or create humorous dog quotations of your own.

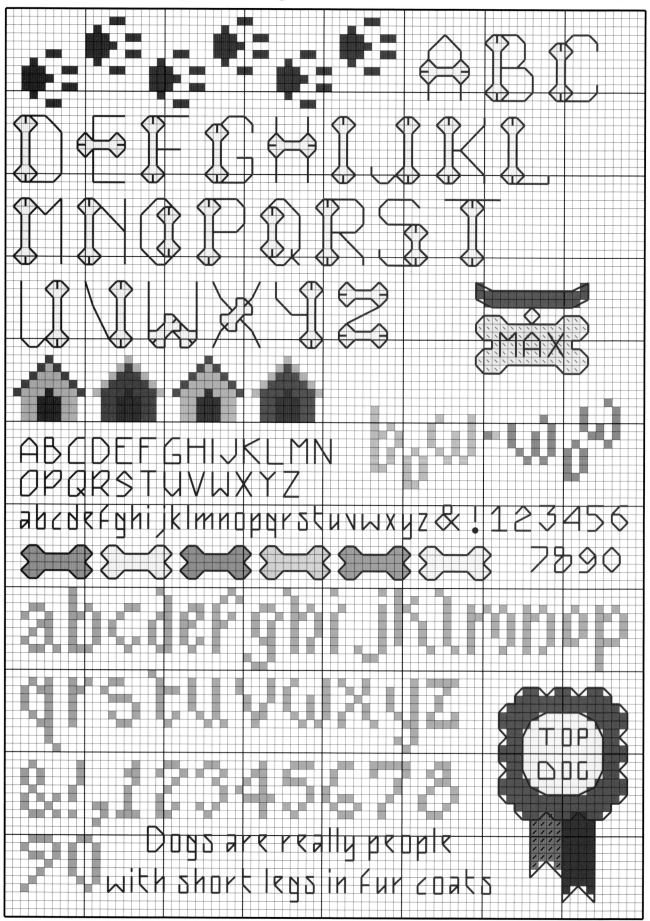

Show the world just how you feel about **you and your dog**.

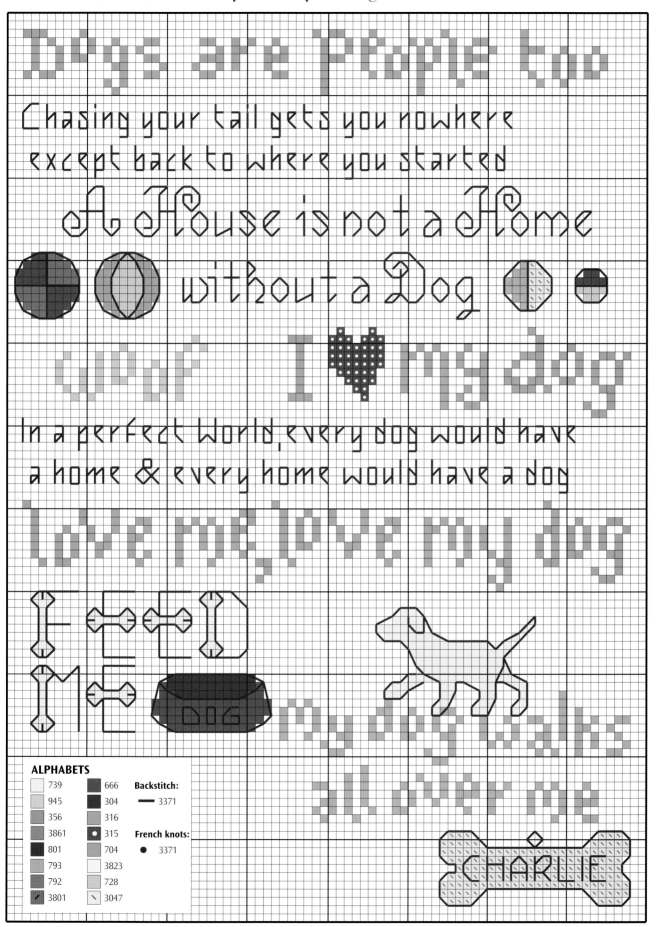

ALPHABETS

739		666	**Backstitch:**		
945		304	— 3371		
356		316			
3861		315			
801		704	**French knots:**		
793		3823	● 3371		
792		728			
3801		3047			

CATS

This chapter is crammed full of wonderful cat designs, their characteristics captured perfectly. Regal cats, playful cats, funny cats, cuddly cats – the sampler opposite gives some idea of the versatility of the many motifs while overleaf you will find ideas for using the designs in a multitude of items. You could display the cats in many more ways: a kitten door hanger for a child's room, a draught excluder adorned with cozy moggies for grandma, a practical paperweight with a favourite cat – the possibilities are endless. The charts feature twelve of the most popular pedigree breeds, including Persians, Orientals, Shorthairs, Bengals and Birmans. Alternate coat colourways are given where appropriate, so if you don't see your cat, it's easy to personalize a design (see page 6). There are charts devoted to lovable 'moggies' and the cutest kittens too. Charted cat-inspired sayings will delight your feline-mad friends and there is a choice of borders, alphabets and motifs so you can personalize your chosen designs.

The Cat Rules!

- I decide what I do, who I live with and what time I eat – dogs have owners but us cats have staff.
- Once I have you trained, I will be affectionate, playful and diverting company.
- I spend almost two-thirds of my life asleep, usually in the warmest place in the house – in a square of sunlight on the carpet or in your lap.

- Grooming takes up about a quarter of my waking time – don't rush me.
- I'm at my most active at dawn and dusk – just when you're not.
- I like to chat loudly in the middle of the night to be sure to get everyone's attention.
- I always give generously: a mouse or bird left on your bed simply says, 'I care'.

The Love of Cats Sampler

This delightful sampler features some of the gorgeous cats and kittens charted in this chapter. The centre of the sampler has a cat saying framed by mice borders but this could easily be changed to one of your own favourite quotes or amusing sayings – see the alphabets on pages 42 and 65. The sampler is stitched on white 14-count Aida using two strands of stranded cotton (floss) for cross stitch and one for backstitch. To plan and stitch your own sampler, refer to page 7.

Stitch count for sampler shown: 146 x 110.
Design size: 26.5 x 20cm (10½ x 7¾in) on 14-count.

Purrfect Presents

Here is a selection of gifts that every cat lover will think are just the cat's whiskers, providing ideas on how to display the many cat designs charted in this chapter. Substitute the designs shown for your favourite cat breed and add a personal touch with names and messages using the phrases and alphabets on pages 64–65. Refer to the list of suppliers on page 104 for the items used.

This square coaster is the ideal item to feature Smokey, the Birman cat (page 53) stitched on 16-count white Aida. Back the embroidery with lightweight iron-on interfacing (see page 100). Trim the fabric edges to fit into an 8.2cm (3¼in) square plastic coaster. Place into the coaster, adding white paper behind the fabric, and then simply assemble the coaster according to the manufacturer's instructions.

Use your own cat or favourite breed, adding the name using the alphabets on page 65. Make sure your design fits into the coaster (see calculating design size page 98). How about a set of coasters featuring each of your cats or a set of your favourite breeds?

Stitch count: 45 x 46.
Design size: 7.3 x 7.3cm (2¾ x 2¾in) on 16-count.

A photograph frame is perfect for the addition of a charming cat motif. This wide suede frame is adorned with an American Shorthair (page 56). Stitch it on 14-count white Aida, then back the embroidery with heavyweight iron-on interfacing (see page 100). Cut around the stitching and stick it on to the frame using PVA glue or double-sided adhesive tape.

Try adding more cats around the frame, choosing the same breed or a mixture, or stitch your own cat and add a panel with their name using one of the alphabets on page 42 or 65.

Stitch count: 22 x 24.
Design size: 4 x 4.3cm
(1½ x 1¾in)
on 14-count.

Stitch count: 30 x 36.
Design size: 5.4 x 6.5cm (2⅛ x 2½in) on 14-count.

A handbag mirror with a portrait of a Persian cat (page 49) would make a lovely gift. Stitch it on 14-count white Aida, then use the rim of the mirror to draw around the design, making sure it is in the centre – the mirror shown is 6cm (2¼in) diameter. Back the finished embroidery with lightweight iron-on interfacing (see page 100). Cut around the design and assemble in the mirror according to the manufacturer's instructions.

Choose another of the cat portraits or stitch any of the cat designs on a fabric with a higher count, which will result in a smaller finished size, i.e., a 16-count or 18-count (see calculating design size page 98).

A baby's bib can display a trio of fluffy Persian kittens (page 49). Ready-made bibs have different sized stitching areas so make sure your design will fit before you begin (see calculating design size page 98). Alternatively, stitch your design on to a piece of Aida, trim it to within 2cm (¾in) of the stitching, turn under the edges and securely stitch the patch to a plain bib. Stitch the baby's name on the bib using one of the alphabets on pages 42 or 65.

Choose one of the small kittens on pages 60–61 or use a quote from pages 62–63, an ideal one being 'It's not easy being this cute!'.

Stitch count:
17 x 43.
Design size:
3 x 7.8cm (1¼ x 3in)
on 14-count.

Stitch count: 43 x 27.
Design size: 7.8 x 5cm (3 x 2in) on 14-count.

Cute greetings cards with a sweet sentiment like this will always raise a smile (page 63). Stitch it on 14-count white Aida, then mount the finished embroidery into a ready-made card with an aperture large enough for the design (see page 101).

Stitch any of the cat designs – perfect for a birthday card, anniversary or someone's special day. To add a personal touch to a card, use one of the alphabets on page 65 to stitch a greeting or name.

This wall hanging displaying an imperious cat (page 63) reminds us of our place in a cat's life. Stitch it on 14-count white Aida with an extra 8cm (3in) top and bottom to fit around the wooden bell pull ends. When the stitching is finished, follow the instructions on page 102 for making up.

Stitch another of the sentiments on pages 62–65 or use any of the cat designs to stitch your own cat or favourite breed, adding your own saying or name using the alphabets on page 65.

Stitch count:
36 x 41.
Design size:
6.5 x 7.5cm
(2½ x 3in) on
14-count.

Persians are glamorous, dignified and decorative – and expecting to be groomed daily.

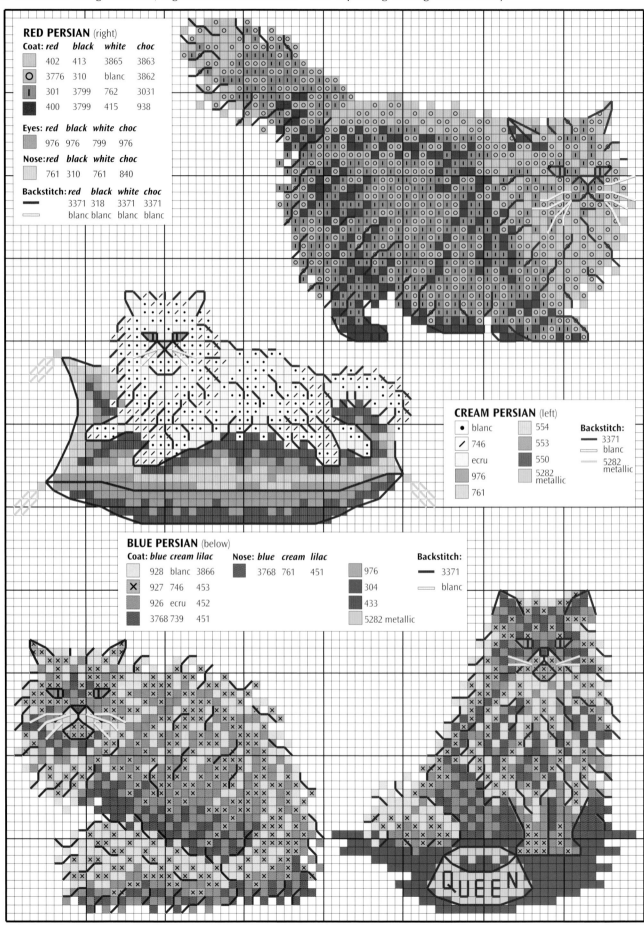

RED PERSIAN (right)

Coat:	red	black	white	choc
	402	413	3865	3863
O	3776	310	blanc	3862
I	301	3799	762	3031
	400	3799	415	938

Eyes:	red	black	white	choc
	976	976	799	976

Nose:	red	black	white	choc
	761	310	761	840

Backstitch:	red	black	white	choc
▬		3371	318	3371	3371
▭		blanc	blanc	blanc	blanc

CREAM PERSIAN (left)

●	blanc			554
╱	746			553
	ecru			550
	976			5282 metallic
	761			

Backstitch:
- ▬ 3371
- ▭ blanc
- ▬ 5282 metallic

BLUE PERSIAN (below)

Coat:	blue	cream	lilac		Nose:	blue	cream	lilac				Backstitch:
	928	blanc	3866			3768	761	451			976	▬ 3371
✕	927	746	453								304	▭ blanc
	926	ecru	452								433	
	3768	739	451								5282 metallic	

Persian point colourings include black, blue, chocolate, cream, golden, lilac, red and white.

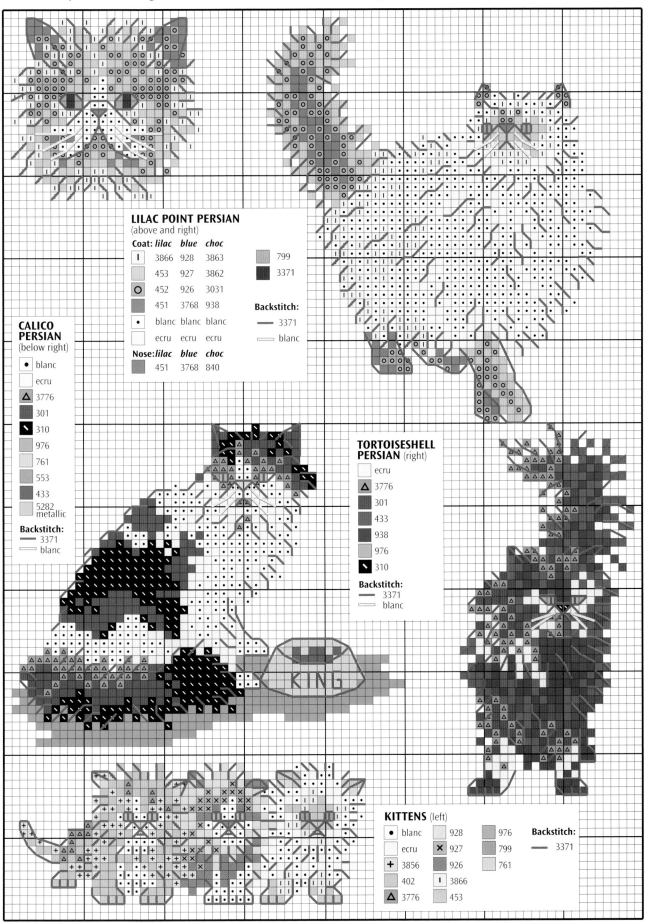

LILAC POINT PERSIAN
(above and right)

Coat:	lilac	blue	choc
I	3866	928	3863
	453	927	3862
O	452	926	3031
	451	3768	938
•	blanc	blanc	blanc
	ecru	ecru	ecru

| | 799 |
| | 3371 |

Backstitch:
— 3371
═ blanc

Nose:	lilac	blue	choc
	451	3768	840

CALICO PERSIAN
(below right)

•	blanc
	ecru
△	3776
	301
◣	310
	976
	761
	553
	433
	5282 metallic

Backstitch:
— 3371
═ blanc

TORTOISESHELL PERSIAN (right)

	ecru
△	3776
	301
	433
	938
	976
◣	310

Backstitch:
— 3371
═ blanc

KITTENS (left)

•	blanc		928		976
	ecru	✕	927		799
+	3856		926		761
	402	I	3866		
△	3776		453		

Backstitch:
— 3371

KING

CATS **49**

The Siamese, also called the Royal Cat of Siam, is a friendly, chatty cat with the most to say.

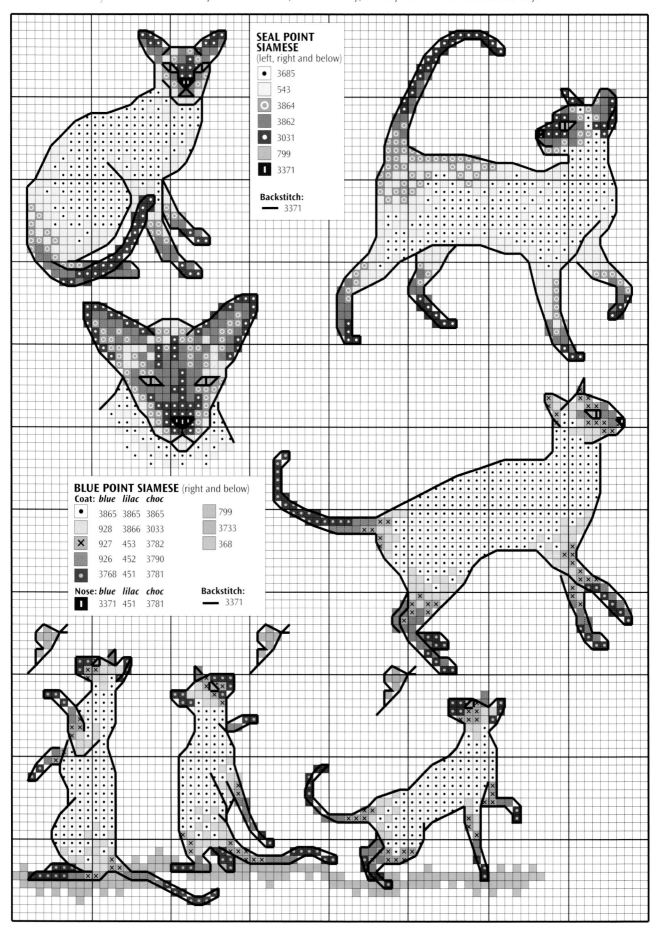

SEAL POINT SIAMESE
(left, right and below)

- 3685
- 543
- 3864
- 3862
- 3031
- 799
- 3371

Backstitch:
— 3371

BLUE POINT SIAMESE (right and below)

Coat:	*blue*	*lilac*	*choc*		
•	3865	3865	3865		799
	928	3866	3033		3733
✕	927	453	3782		368
	926	452	3790		
	3768	451	3781		

Nose:	*blue*	*lilac*	*choc*
▐	3371	451	3781

Backstitch:
— 3371

With ancestors from Siam, the Oriental Shorthair is outrageously but endearingly attention seeking.

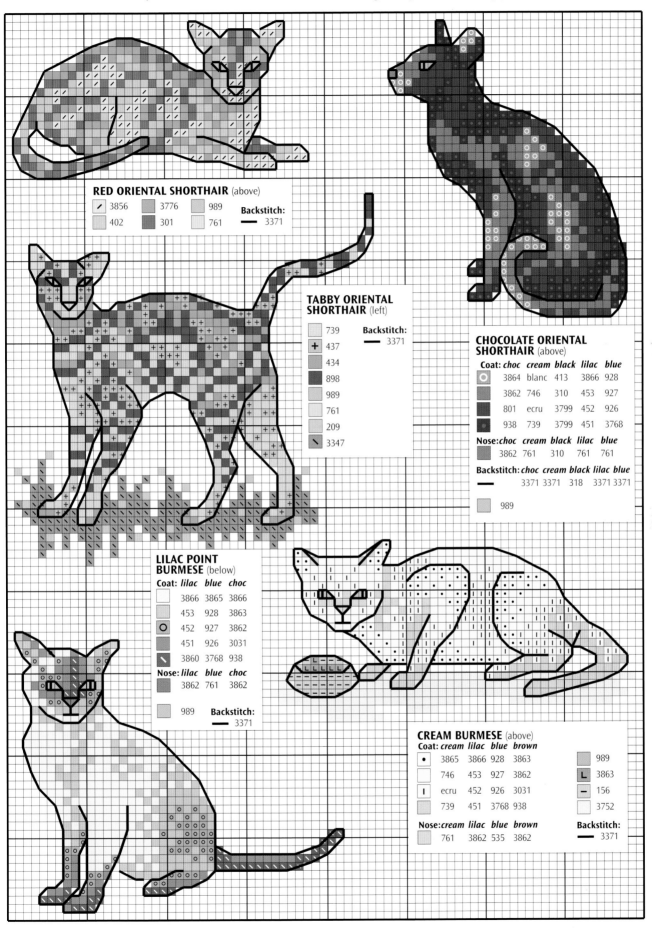

RED ORIENTAL SHORTHAIR (above)

✓	3856	3776		989	
	402	301		761	

Backstitch:
— 3371

TABBY ORIENTAL SHORTHAIR (left)

		Backstitch:
	739	— 3371
+	437	
	434	
	898	
	989	
	761	
	209	
╲	3347	

CHOCOLATE ORIENTAL SHORTHAIR (above)

Coat:	choc	cream	black	lilac	blue
⊙	3864	blanc	413	3866	928
	3862	746	310	453	927
	801	ecru	3799	452	926
⊙	938	739	3799	451	3768

Nose:	choc	cream	black	lilac	blue
	3862	761	310	761	761

Backstitch:	choc	cream	black	lilac	blue
—		3371	3371	318	3371	3371

	989

LILAC POINT BURMESE (below)

Coat:	lilac	blue	choc
	3866	3865	3866
	453	928	3863
○	452	927	3862
	451	926	3031
╲	3860	3768	938

Nose:	lilac	blue	choc
	3862	761	3862

		Backstitch:
	989	— 3371

CREAM BURMESE (above)

Coat:	cream	lilac	blue	brown		
•	3865	3866	928	3863		989
	746	453	927	3862	L	3863
I	ecru	452	926	3031	—	156
	739	451	3768	938		3752

Nose:	cream	lilac	blue	brown	Backstitch:
	761	3862	535	3862	— 3371

The Exotic Shorthair is as dignified as its ancestor, the Persian, but with a lively, playful side.

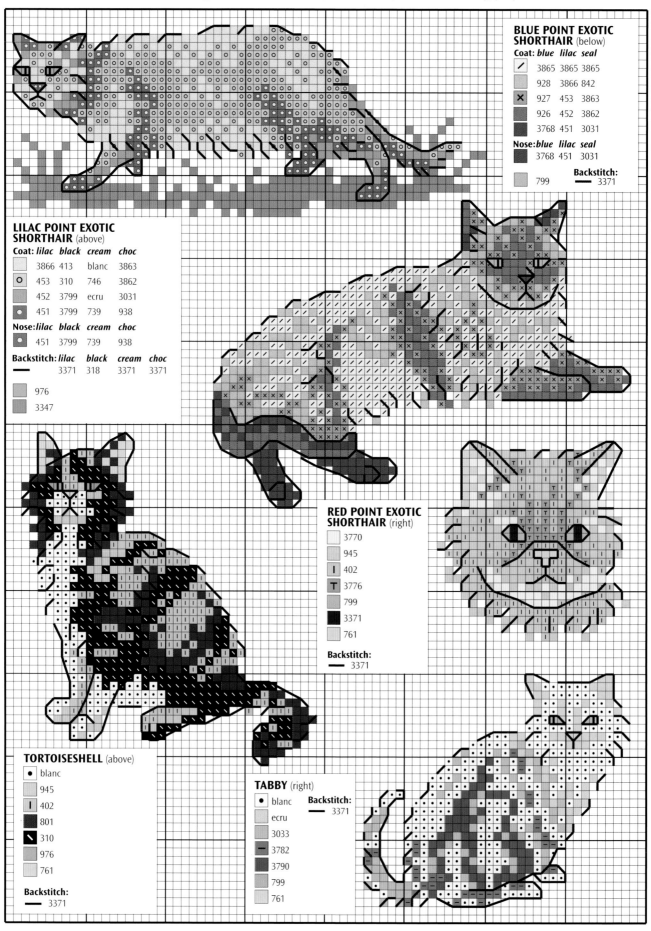

BLUE POINT EXOTIC SHORTHAIR (below)

Coat:	blue	lilac	seal
╱	3865	3865	3865
	928	3866	842
✕	927	453	3863
	926	452	3862
	3768	451	3031

Nose:	blue	lilac	seal
	3768	451	3031

		Backstitch:
	799	— 3371

LILAC POINT EXOTIC SHORTHAIR (above)

Coat:	lilac	black	cream	choc
	3866	413	blanc	3863
○	453	310	746	3862
	452	3799	ecru	3031
•	451	3799	739	938

Nose:	lilac	black	cream	choc
•	451	3799	739	938

Backstitch:	lilac	black	cream	choc
—		3371	318	3371	3371

	976
	3347

RED POINT EXOTIC SHORTHAIR (right)

	3770
	945
I	402
T	3776
	799
	3371
	761

Backstitch:
— 3371

TORTOISESHELL (above)

•	blanc
	945
I	402
	801
	310
	976
	761

Backstitch:
— 3371

TABBY (right)

•	blanc
	ecru
	3033
—	3782
	3790
	799
	761

Backstitch:
— 3371

52 CATS

The Birman is the sacred temple cat of Burma, with distinctive white feet and a gentle, loving nature.

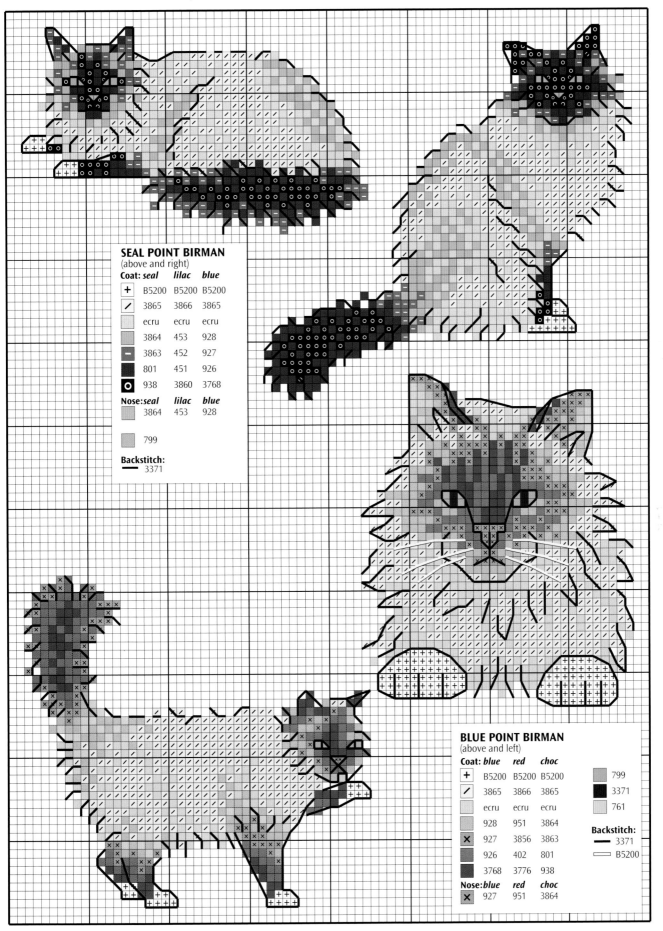

SEAL POINT BIRMAN
(above and right)

Coat:	seal	lilac	blue
+	B5200	B5200	B5200
/	3865	3866	3865
	ecru	ecru	ecru
	3864	453	928
−	3863	452	927
	801	451	926
⊙	938	3860	3768

Nose:	seal	lilac	blue
	3864	453	928
		799	

Backstitch:
— 3371

BLUE POINT BIRMAN
(above and left)

Coat:	blue	red	choc		
+	B5200	B5200	B5200		799
/	3865	3866	3865		3371
	ecru	ecru	ecru		761
	928	951	3864		
✕	927	3856	3863		**Backstitch:**
	926	402	801		— 3371
	3768	3776	938		▭ B5200

Nose:	blue	red	choc
✕	927	951	3864

The **Maine Coon** is a gentle giant with feathered lynx-like ears and is a skilful hunter.

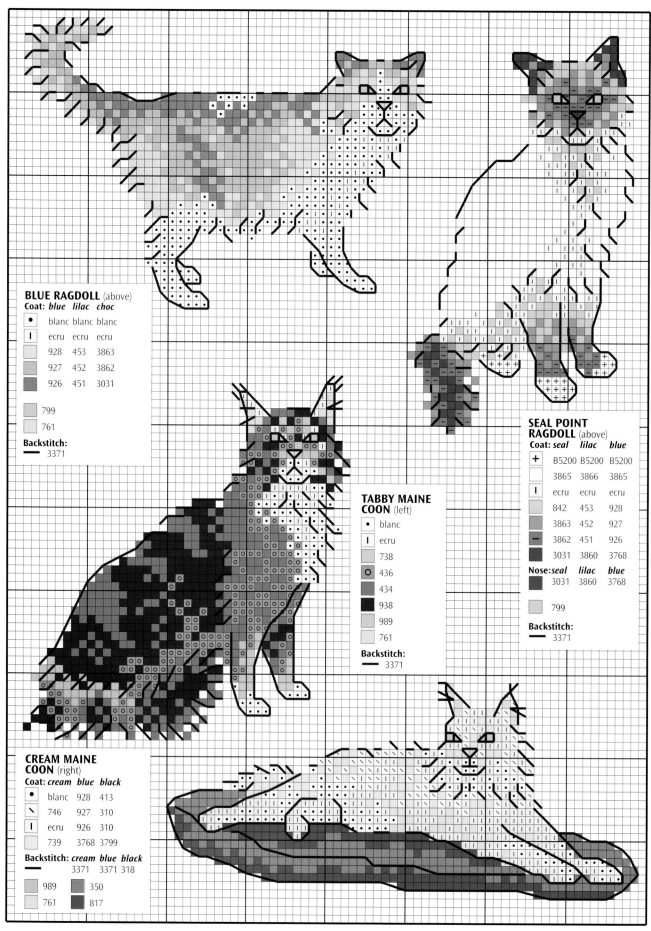

BLUE RAGDOLL (above)
Coat: *blue lilac choc*

•	blanc	blanc	blanc
I	ecru	ecru	ecru
	928	453	3863
	927	452	3862
	926	451	3031
	799		
	761		

Backstitch:
—— 3371

TABBY MAINE COON (left)

•	blanc
I	ecru
	738
O	436
	434
	938
	989
	761

Backstitch:
—— 3371

SEAL POINT RAGDOLL (above)
Coat: *seal lilac blue*

+	B5200	B5200	B5200
	3865	3866	3865
I	ecru	ecru	ecru
	842	453	928
	3863	452	927
−	3862	451	926
	3031	3860	3768

Nose: *seal lilac blue*

	3031	3860	3768
	799		

Backstitch:
—— 3371

CREAM MAINE COON (right)
Coat: *cream blue black*

•	blanc	928	413
\	746	927	310
I	ecru	926	310
	739	3768	3799

Backstitch: *cream blue black*
              3371 3371 318

	989		350
	761		817

54 CATS

Descended from the wild cats of Asia, the Bengal still bears the most fabulously patterned coat.

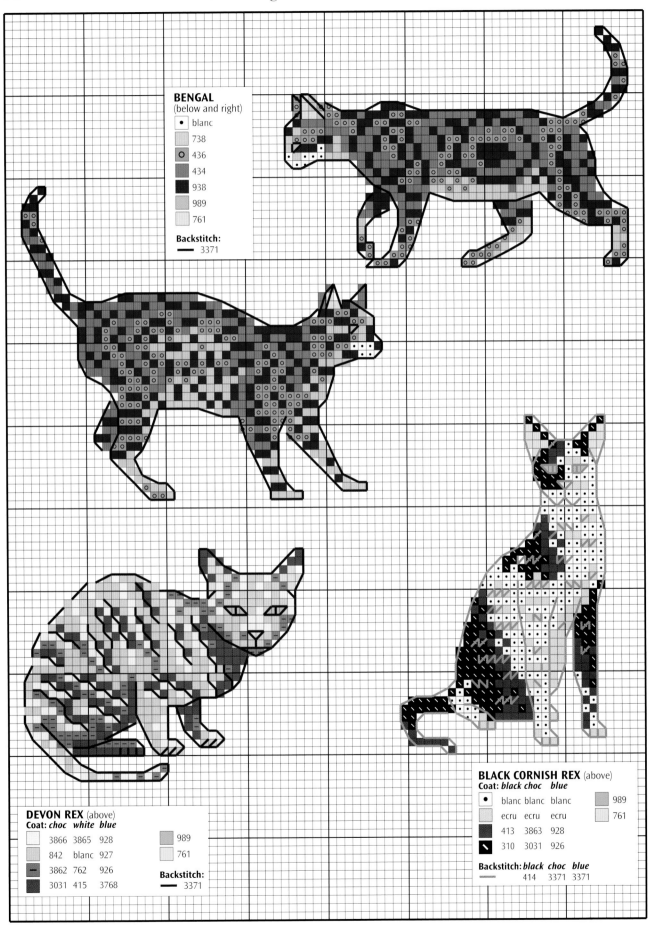

BENGAL
(below and right)

•	blanc
	738
O	436
	434
	938
	989
	761

Backstitch:
—— 3371

DEVON REX (above)
Coat: *choc* *white* *blue*

	3866	3865	928
	842	blanc	927
-	3862	762	926
	3031	415	3768

	989
	761

Backstitch:
—— 3371

BLACK CORNISH REX (above)
Coat: *black choc* *blue*

•	blanc	blanc	blanc		989
	ecru	ecru	ecru		761
	413	3863	928		
\	310	3031	926		

Backstitch: *black choc blue*
—————— 414 3371 3371

The domestic cat of America, the American Shorthair probably arrived with the Pilgrim Fathers.

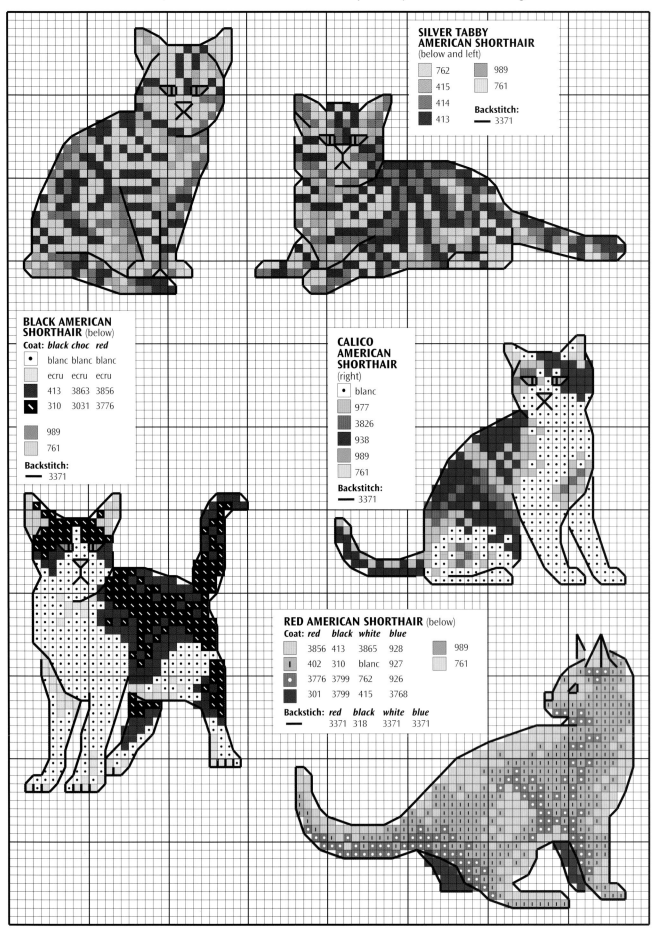

SILVER TABBY AMERICAN SHORTHAIR
(below and left)

	762		989
	415		761
	414		
	413	**Backstitch:**	
		—	3371

BLACK AMERICAN SHORTHAIR (below)

Coat:	*black*	*choc*	*red*
•	blanc	blanc	blanc
	ecru	ecru	ecru
	413	3863	3856
◣	310	3031	3776
	989		
	761		

Backstitch:
— 3371

CALICO AMERICAN SHORTHAIR (right)

•	blanc
	977
	3826
	938
	989
	761

Backstitch:
— 3371

RED AMERICAN SHORTHAIR (below)

Coat:	*red*	*black*	*white*	*blue*		
	3856	413	3865	928		989
I	402	310	blanc	927		761
•	3776	3799	762	926		
	301	3799	415	3768		

Backstich: | *red* | *black* | *white* | *blue* |
— | 3371 | 318 | 3371 | 3371 |

The British Shorthair arrived in Britain with the Romans and is the national cat of the British Isles.

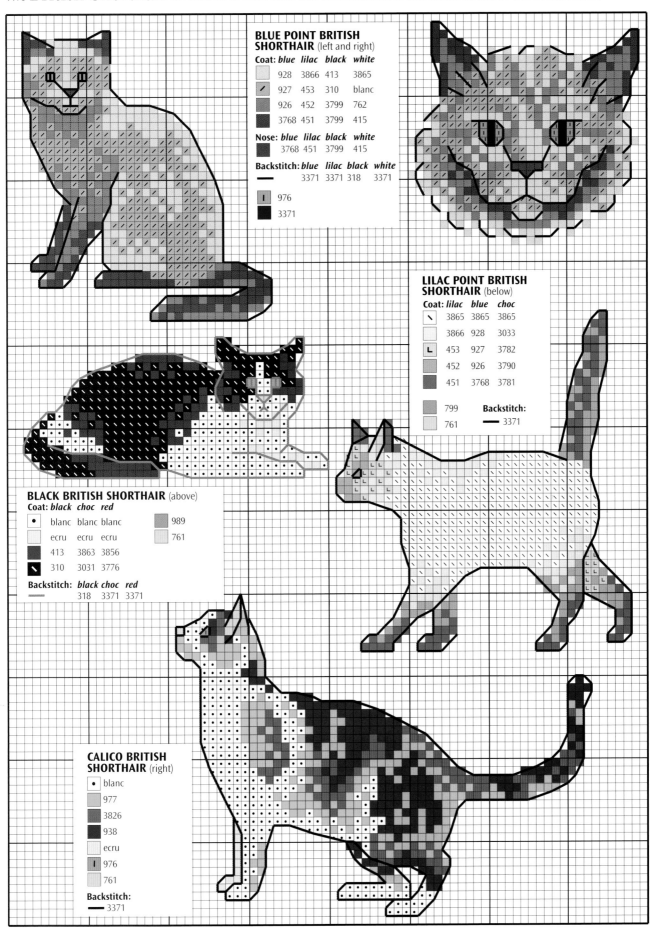

BLUE POINT BRITISH SHORTHAIR (left and right)

Coat:	blue	lilac	black	white
	928	3866	413	3865
✓	927	453	310	blanc
	926	452	3799	762
	3768	451	3799	415

Nose:	blue	lilac	black	white
	3768	451	3799	415

Backstitch:	blue	lilac	black	white
—		3371	3371	318	3371

I	976
	3371

LILAC POINT BRITISH SHORTHAIR (below)

Coat:	lilac	blue	choc
＼	3865	3865	3865
	3866	928	3033
L	453	927	3782
	452	926	3790
	451	3768	3781

	799	**Backstitch:**
	761	— 3371

BLACK BRITISH SHORTHAIR (above)

Coat:	black	choc	red
•	blanc	blanc	blanc
	ecru	ecru	ecru
	413	3863	3856
＼	310	3031	3776

	989
	761

Backstitch:	black	choc	red
—		318	3371	3371

CALICO BRITISH SHORTHAIR (right)

•	blanc
	977
	3826
	938
	ecru
I	976
	761

Backstitch:
— 3371

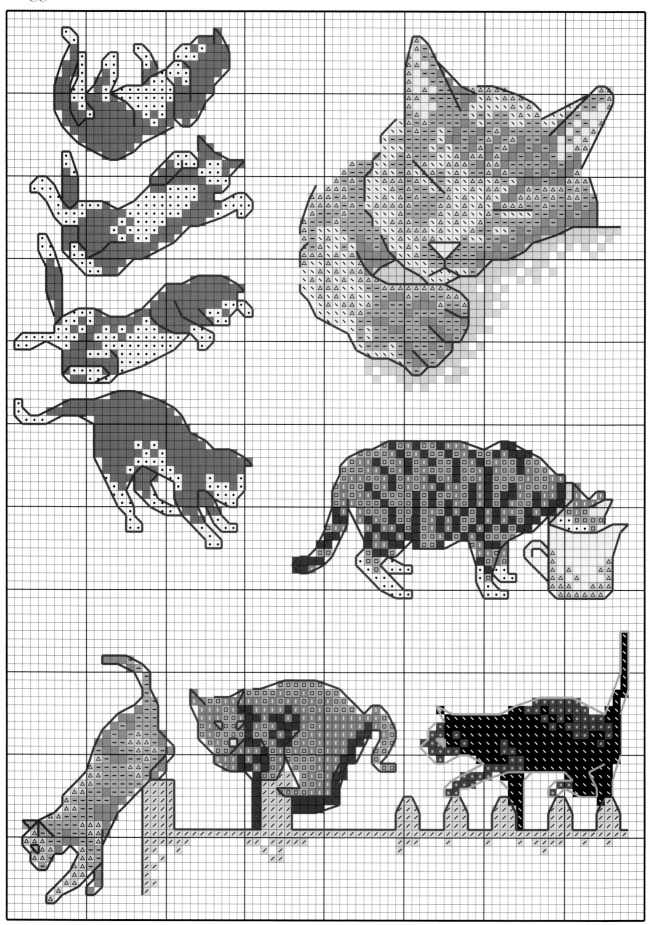

A cat doesn't need a pedigree to become a well-loved part of the family – **mixed breeds** are magic too!

MOGGIES

•	blanc		989
	ecru		761
+	3856	╱	842
	402	I	758
	3776		3821
□	3863		162
I	3862		
	3031	**Backstitch:**	
╲	3866	──	3371
△	453	─ ─	648
−	452		
	451		
	415		
✕	414		
	3799		
◣	310		
	738		
○	436		
	434		
	801		

FIVE CATS ON FENCE AND WALL (including two cats bottom opposite page)
(if working all five cats in a sequence, stitch from left to right, matching the fence level)

Playful kittens are learning to hunt, without another cat to stalk, toys, balls of wool and bees will do.

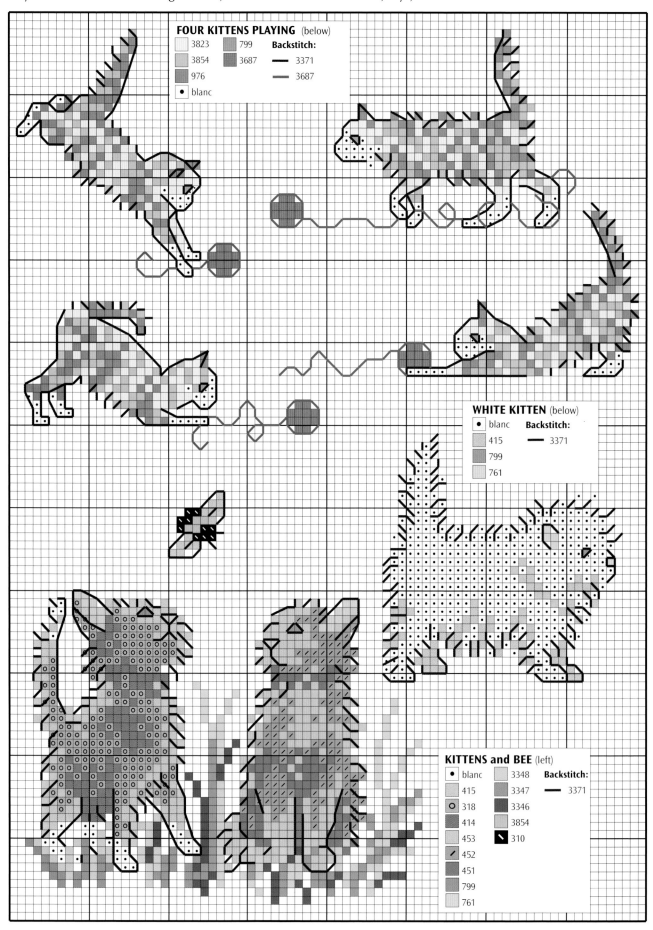

FOUR KITTENS PLAYING (below)

	3823		799	**Backstitch:**
	3854		3687	— 3371
	976			— 3687
•	blanc			

WHITE KITTEN (below)

•	blanc	**Backstitch:**
	415	— 3371
	799	
	761	

KITTENS and BEE (left)

•	blanc		3348	**Backstitch:**
	415		3347	— 3371
○	318		3346	
	414		3854	
	453		310	
╱	452			
	451			
	799			
	761			

The cutest of kittens are sure to enhance any gift or card.

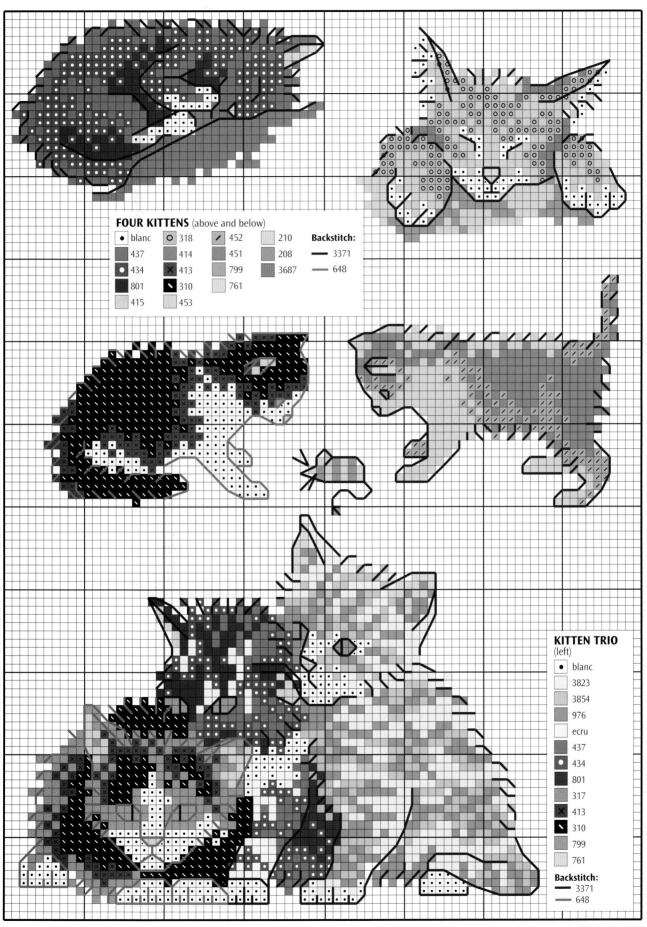

FOUR KITTENS (above and below)

• blanc	○ 318	╱ 452	210
437	414	451	208
⊙ 434	✕ 413	799	3687
801	◣ 310	761	
415	453		

Backstitch:
—— 3371
—— 648

KITTEN TRIO
(left)

• blanc	
	3823
	3854
	976
	ecru
	437
⊙	434
	801
	317
✕	413
◣	310
	799
	761

Backstitch:
—— 3371
—— 648

You are sure to find many uses for these humorous sayings and fun motifs.

Cat's motto
Whatever
you've done
wrong...

a spoilt cat lives
here

always make
it look like
the dog did it

SLEEP ✓
EAT ✓
SLEEP ✓
SLEEP

My cat is

PURR-FECT!

Best friends never
fight like cats & dogs

SENTIMENTS

• blanc		415		554	**French knots:**	
ecru		318		553	● 3371	
＼ 739		3856		792		
✕ 738	+	402		321	**Backstitch:**	
437		3776		3325	▬ 3371	
✒ 436	I	301		996	▭ blanc	
434	−	160		304		
◉ 433	◥	310	▵	3046		
▬ 898		989		3047		
453		799		3045		
◯ 452		761		5284 metallic		
762						

These fitting cat quotations are bound to raise a smile.

People who hate cats
will come back as mice

I purr
therefore I am

beware of
the kitten

It's not easy

being this cute!

the best things
in life are
FURRY

Cats were
once
worshipped
as gods...
Cats have never
forgotten
this

These cat quotes would be great featured in a cat sampler.

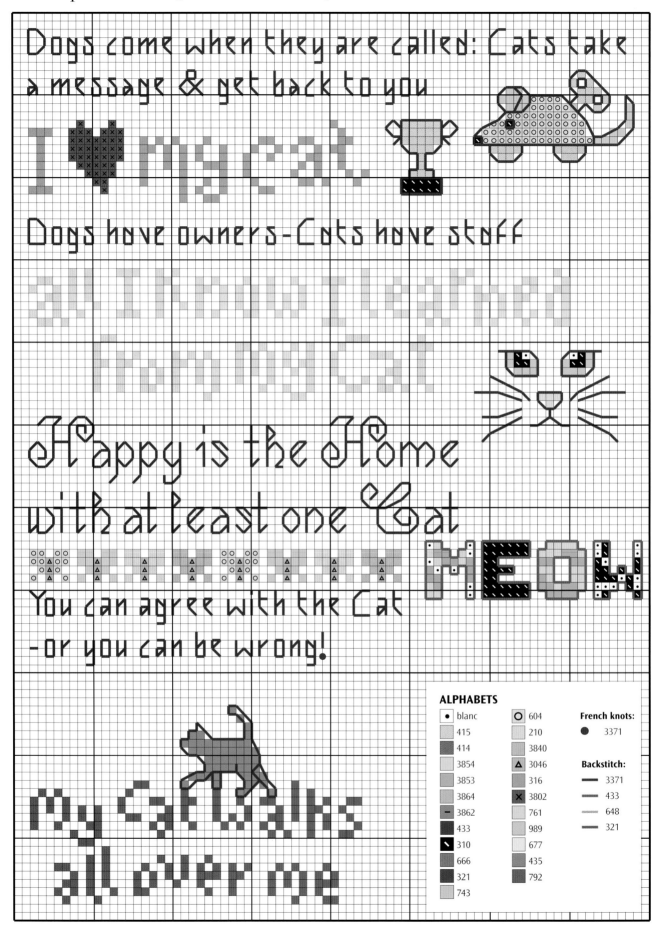

Dogs come when they are called: Cats take a message & get back to you

I ♥ my cat

Dogs have owners - Cats have staff

all I have learned from my cat

Happy is the Home with at least one Cat

MEOW

You can agree with the Cat - or you can be wrong!

My Cat Walks all over me

ALPHABETS

•	blanc	○	604
	415		210
	414		3840
	3854	△	3046
	3853		316
	3864	✕	3802
–	3862		761
	433		989
◪	310		677
	666		435
	321		792
	743		

French knots:
● 3371

Backstitch:
— 3371
— 433
— 648
— 321

Use these amusing alphabets to personalize gifts and cards or create cat sayings or poems of your own.

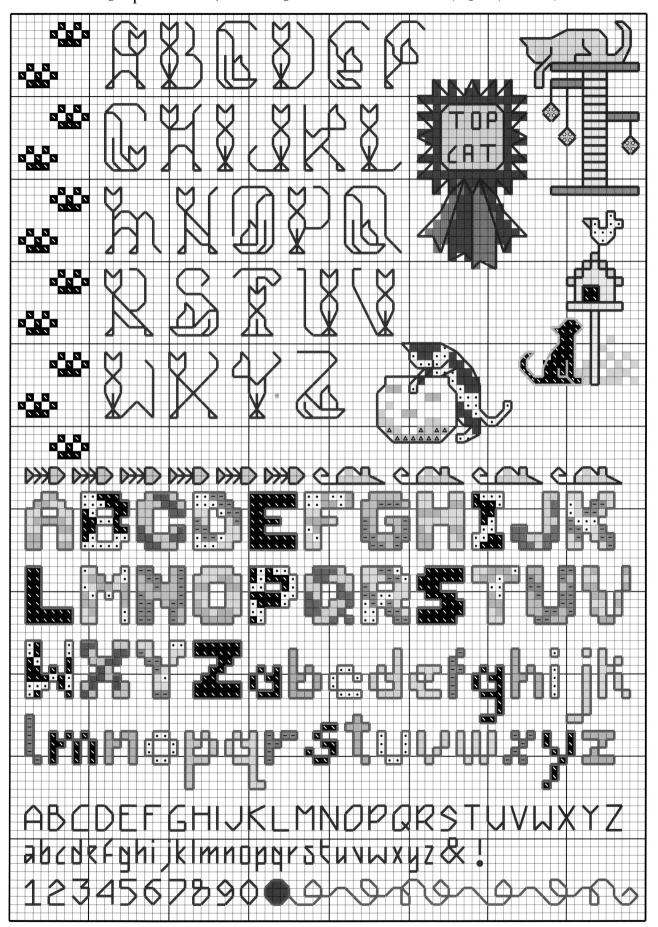

FURRY FRIENDS

Small mammals such as hamsters, gerbils, rats and mice are often called pocket pets as they love to find dark, snug places for a nap. There's never a dull moment with pets like these as they are natural escape artists – even the sleepiest hamster will seize an opportunity for adventure. The ten pages of charts in this chapter include rabbits, guinea pigs and those chief mischief-makers, ferrets, with alternative coat colours given where appropriate. There are also designs for more unusual pets like chinchillas, degus and chipmunks. You will see from the project ideas on these pages that the designs perfectly capture the characteristics of these animals – from tumbling rats on a pen holder to a cheeky ferret stealing treats from a storage jar.

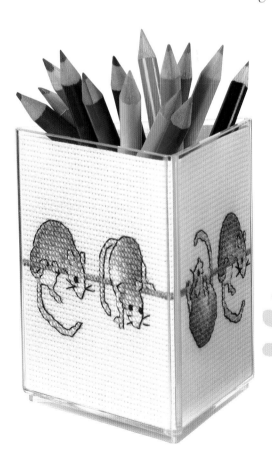

This pen holder

has three sides to display a row of delightful tumbling rats (page 74). Each part of the design is stitched on 14-count white Aida using two strands of stranded cotton (floss) for cross stitch and one for backstitch. Using lines of tacking (basting) divide the Aida into three sections each 46 squares wide. Mark the centre of each section. In the first section, stitch the first and second rats, in the next section stitch the third and first rats, and in the final section stitch the second and third rats. Make sure the two rats are centralized in each section. Join them together with a line of brown cross stitches. Back the stitching with iron-on interfacing (see page 100). Measure the height of the pen holder and cut the fabric around the stitching to fit, making sure the rats are centralized. Place inside the pen holder and assemble according to the manufacturer's instructions. Each side of the pen holder is 8.2 x 9.5cm (3¼ x 3¾in).

Bring a child's pet into the bedroom by decorating their bed linen. Work a long repeating border of mice along a long length of Aida band, hem each end and then sew the band to the border of a sheet or pillowcase.

Stitch count: 22 x 138.
Design size: 4 x 25cm (1½ x 10in) on 14-count.

A hanging cushion featuring three delightful degus (page 73) makes a lovely little gift. It is stitched over two fabric threads of 28-count evenweave using two strands of stranded cotton (floss) for cross stitch and one for backstitch. Use the alphabet on page 65 to work each letter in a single colour, using DMC 839, 840, 841 randomly. Making up instructions for the cushion are on page 103.

Instead of degu, use your own pet, perhaps a snoozing rabbit, or stitch a sign for a sleepy friend. Instead of stuffing the hanging you could fill it with sweet-smelling pot-pourri.

Stitch count: 40 x 46.
Design size: 7.2 x 8.3cm (2¾ x 3¼in) on 28-count.

Stitch count: 27 x 99.
Design size: 5 x 18cm (2 x 7in) on 14-count.

A name plate for a child's bedroom door showing off their pet gerbils (page 71) is sure to be appreciated. It is stitched on 14-count cream Aida using two strands of stranded cotton (floss) for cross stitch and one for backstitch. When stitching is completed, back it with iron-on interfacing (see page 100) and mount into a ready-made door plate according to the manufacturer's instructions. The door plate used is 6 x 26cm (2¼ x 10¼in).

You could add the child's name using the alphabet on page 42 and stitch their own pet instead of the gerbils (see calculating design size page 98).

This useful ruler is perfect for fitting a snug trio of running guinea pigs (page 70). They are stitched on 14-count white Aida using two strands of stranded cotton (floss) for cross stitch and one for the backstitch. When the stitching is completed, mount into a ready-made 15cm (6in) long ruler according to the manufacturer's instructions.

For someone whose pet passion is guinea pigs or gerbils, there are lots of designs to choose from on pages 70–71, so why not work a set of four framed pictures to decorate a study or bedroom wall?

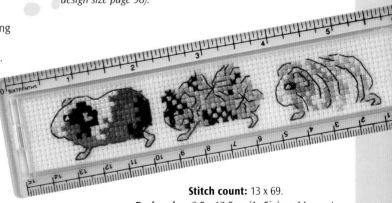

Stitch count: 13 x 69.
Design size: 2.5 x 12.5cm (1x 5in) on 14-count.

Stitch count: 48 x 36.
Design size: 8.7 x 6.5cm (3½ x 2½in) on 14-count.

A storage jar might stop Bandit getting at these tasty treats, but perhaps not? Bandit (page 76) is stitched on 14-count white Aida using two strands of stranded cotton (floss) for cross stitch and one for backstitch. The words are worked using DMC 3807 and the alphabet on page 42. Back the patch with iron-on interfacing (see page 100) and stick it on to the jar using double-sided adhesive tape or PVA glue.

The ferret designs on pages 76–77 would make fun birthday cards – simply add a greeting using the backstitch alphabet on page 65 and mount into a ready-made card (see page 101).

With their soft fur, twitching noses and pretty eyes, **rabbits** are just impossible to resist.

543	I	739	
842		437	
840	▲	435	
839		761	
• blanc		760	
O 762	•	433	
415		3348	
− 318		3347	
413	✕	3821	
✓ 3865		3840	

Backstitch:

The English Spot loves to jump and run, while the Dutch has striking markings on its short lustrous fur.

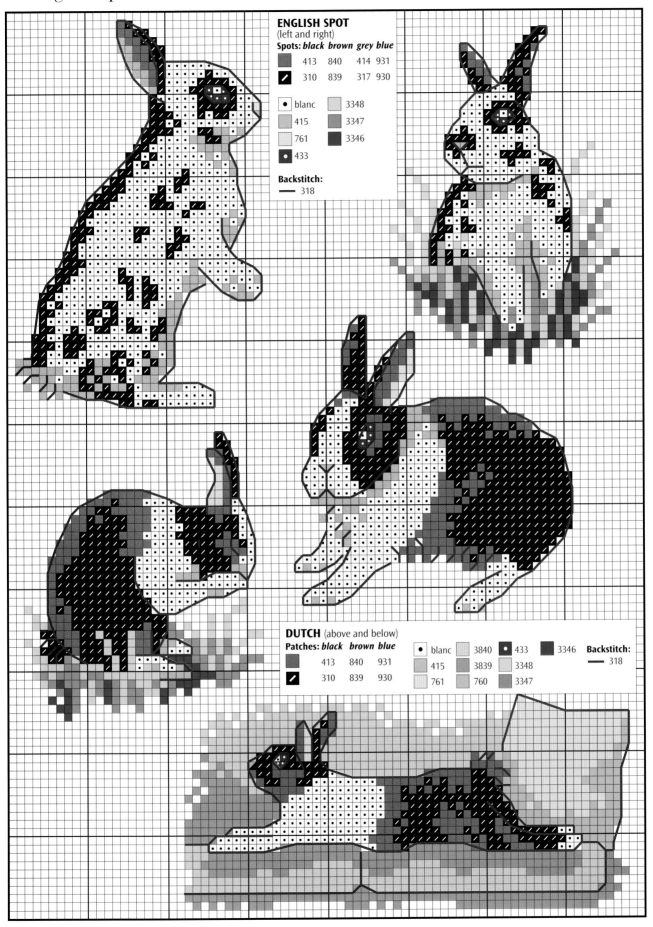

ENGLISH SPOT
(left and right)
Spots: *black brown grey blue*

	413	840	414	931
	310	839	317	930

• blanc			3348
	415		3347
	761		3346
	433		

Backstitch:
— 318

DUTCH (above and below)
Patches: *black brown blue*

	413	840	931	• blanc		3840		433		3346
	310	839	930		415		3839		3348
					761		760		3347

Backstitch:
— 318

A guinea pig, or cavy, will let you know when it is hungry with loud squeaks, snorts and whistles.

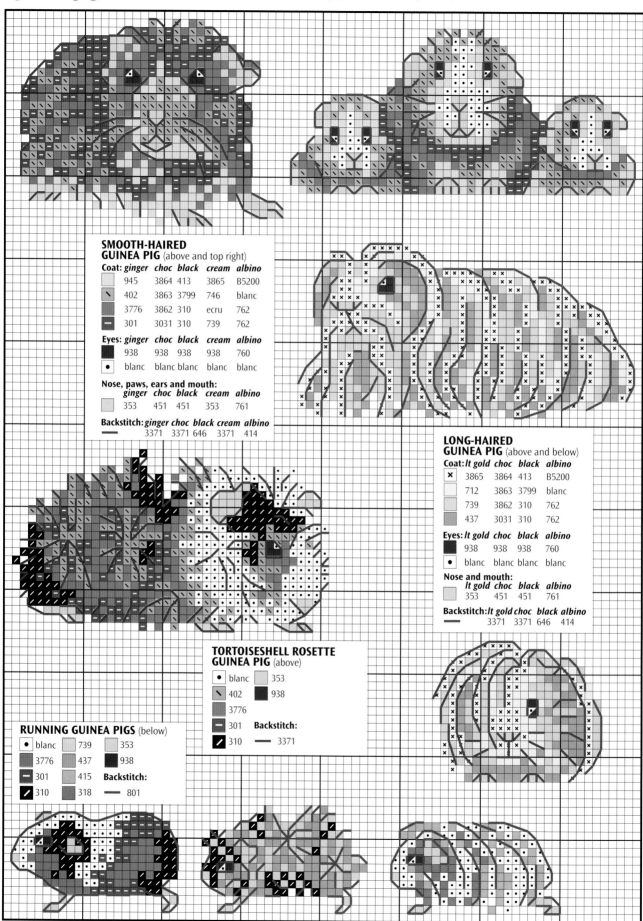

SMOOTH-HAIRED GUINEA PIG (above and top right)

Coat:	ginger	choc	black	cream	albino
	945	3864	413	3865	B5200
	402	3863	3799	746	blanc
	3776	3862	310	ecru	762
	301	3031	310	739	762

Eyes:	ginger	choc	black	cream	albino
	938	938	938	938	760
•	blanc	blanc	blanc	blanc	blanc

Nose, paws, ears and mouth:

	ginger	choc	black	cream	albino
	353	451	451	353	761

Backstitch:	ginger	choc	black	cream	albino
—		3371	3371	646	3371	414

LONG-HAIRED GUINEA PIG (above and below)

Coat:	lt gold	choc	black	albino
×	3865	3864	413	B5200
	712	3863	3799	blanc
	739	3862	310	762
	437	3031	310	762

Eyes:	lt gold	choc	black	albino
	938	938	938	760
•	blanc	blanc	blanc	blanc

Nose and mouth:

	lt gold	choc	black	albino
	353	451	451	761

Backstitch:	lt gold	choc	black	albino
—		3371	3371	646	414

TORTOISESHELL ROSETTE GUINEA PIG (above)

•	blanc		353
	402		938
	3776		
—	301		Backstitch:
	310	—	3371

RUNNING GUINEA PIGS (below)

•	blanc		739		353
	3776		437		938
—	301		415		Backstitch:
	310		318	—	801

Hamsters sleep soundly but may wake in a grumpy mood; gerbils are easy to keep and love running in a wheel.

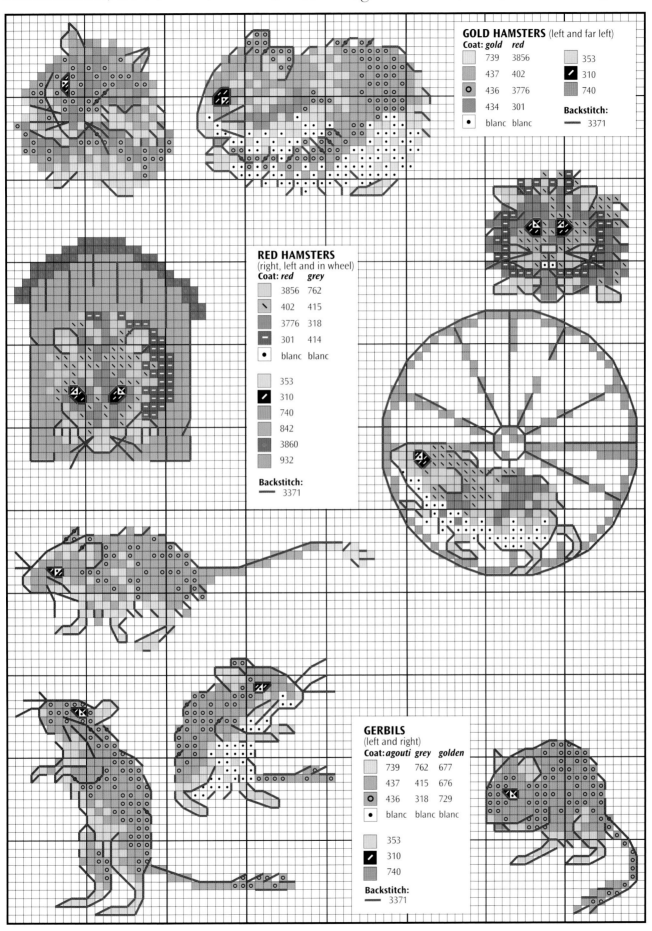

GOLD HAMSTERS (left and far left)

Coat:	*gold*	*red*		
	739	3856		353
	437	402		310
○	436	3776		740
	434	301		
•	blanc	blanc		

Backstitch:
— 3371

RED HAMSTERS
(right, left and in wheel)

Coat:	*red*	*grey*
	3856	762
\	402	415
	3776	318
—	301	414
•	blanc	blanc
	353	
	310	
	740	
	842	
	3860	
	932	

Backstitch:
— 3371

GERBILS
(left and right)

Coat:	*agouti*	*grey*	*golden*
	739	762	677
	437	415	676
○	436	318	729
•	blanc	blanc	blanc
	353		
	310		
	740		

Backstitch:
— 3371

FURRY FRIENDS **71**

Chinchillas love rolling around in a dust bath; it cleans their luxurious fur, as well as being great fun.

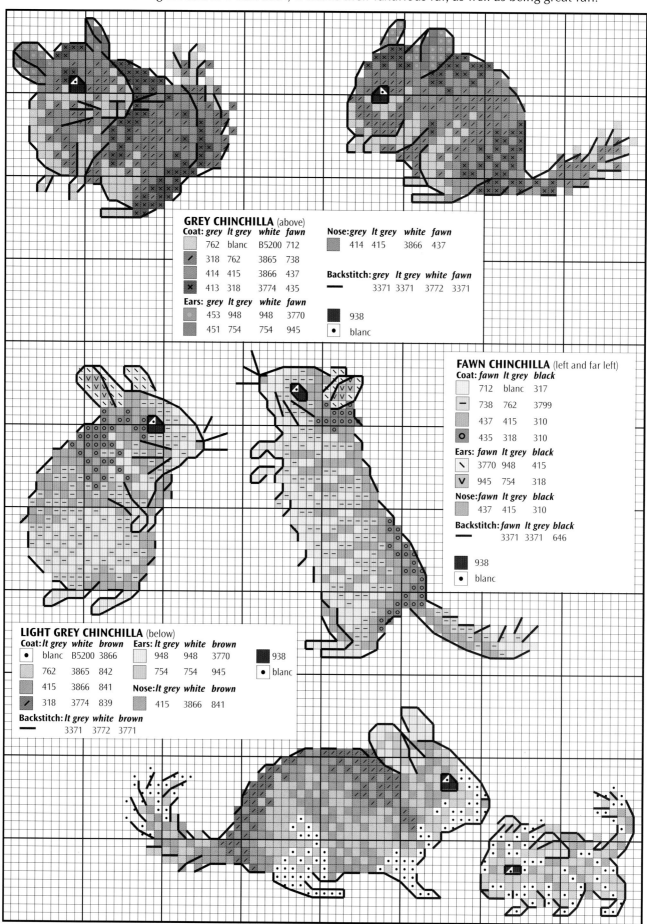

GREY CHINCHILLA (above)

Coat:	grey	lt grey	white	fawn
	762	blanc	B5200	712
╱	318	762	3865	738
	414	415	3866	437
✕	413	318	3774	435

Ears:	grey	lt grey	white	fawn
	453	948	948	3770
	451	754	754	945

Nose:	grey	lt grey	white	fawn
	414	415	3866	437

Backstitch:	grey	lt grey	white	fawn
—	3371	3371	3772	3371

	938
•	blanc

FAWN CHINCHILLA (left and far left)

Coat:	fawn	lt grey	black
	712	blanc	317
—	738	762	3799
	437	415	310
◎	435	318	310

Ears:	fawn	lt grey	black
╲	3770	948	415
V	945	754	318

Nose:	fawn	lt grey	black
	437	415	310

Backstitch:	fawn	lt grey	black
—	3371	3371	646

	938
•	blanc

LIGHT GREY CHINCHILLA (below)

Coat:	lt grey	white	brown
•	blanc	B5200	3866
	762	3865	842
	415	3866	841
╱	318	3774	839

Ears:	lt grey	white	brown
	948	948	3770
	754	754	945

Nose:	lt grey	white	brown
	415	3866	841

	938
•	blanc

Backstitch:	lt grey	white	brown
—	3371	3772	3771

Degus are sociable creatures that need to live in groups and sleep in furry piles; chipmunks are friendly and agile.

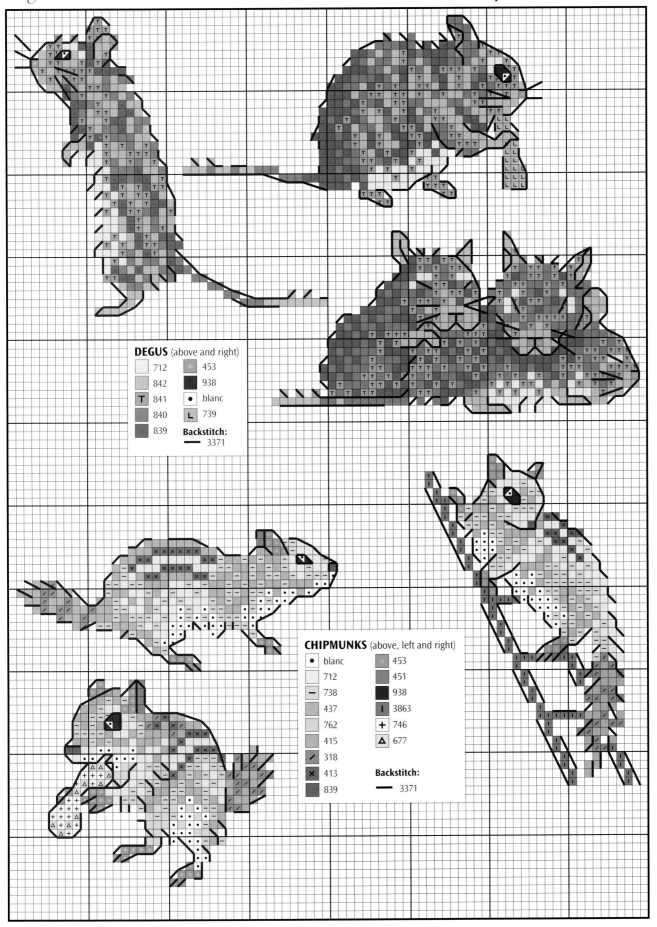

DEGUS (above and right)

	712		453
	842		938
T	841	•	blanc
	840	L	739
	839		

Backstitch:
— 3371

CHIPMUNKS (above, left and right)

•	blanc		453
	712		451
–	738		938
	437	I	3863
	762	+	746
	415	△	677
◢	318		
✕	413	**Backstitch:**	
	839	—	3371

Rats love exploring, so build them their own playground or they'll make one out of your home!

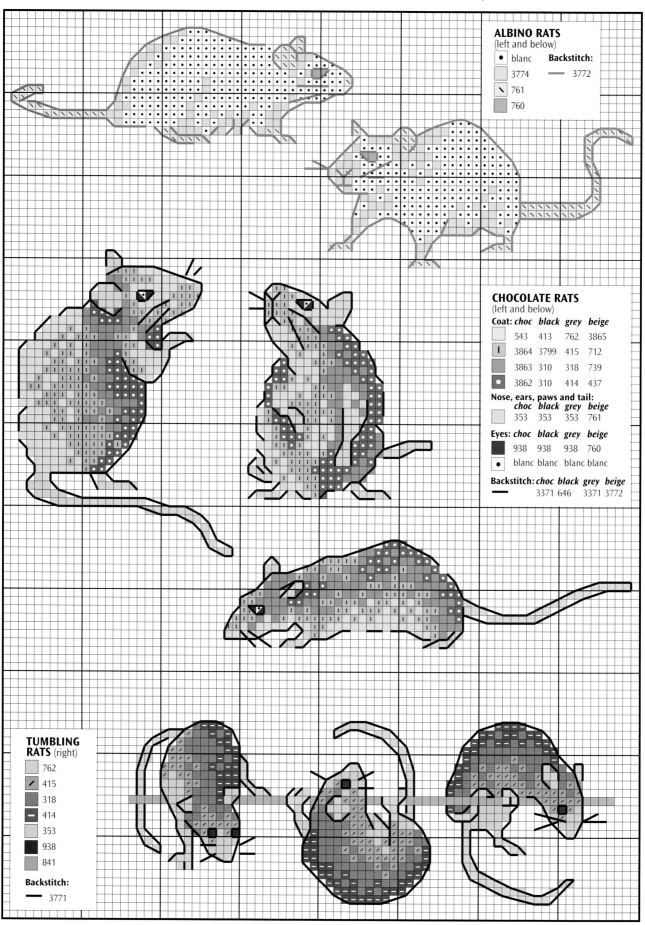

ALBINO RATS
(left and below)

•	blanc	**Backstitch:**
	3774	— 3772
╲	761	
	760	

CHOCOLATE RATS
(left and below)

Coat:
	choc	*black*	*grey*	*beige*
	543	413	762	3865
I	3864	3799	415	712
	3863	310	318	739
•	3862	310	414	437

Nose, ears, paws and tail:
	choc	*black*	*grey*	*beige*
	353	353	353	761

Eyes:
	choc	*black*	*grey*	*beige*
	938	938	938	760
•	blanc	blanc	blanc	blanc

Backstitch:
	choc	*black*	*grey*	*beige*
—		3371	646	3371	3772

TUMBLING RATS (right)

	762
╲	415
	318
—	414
	353
	938
	841

Backstitch:
— 3771

Mice are the smallest pocket pets – active, inquisitive and easily lost.

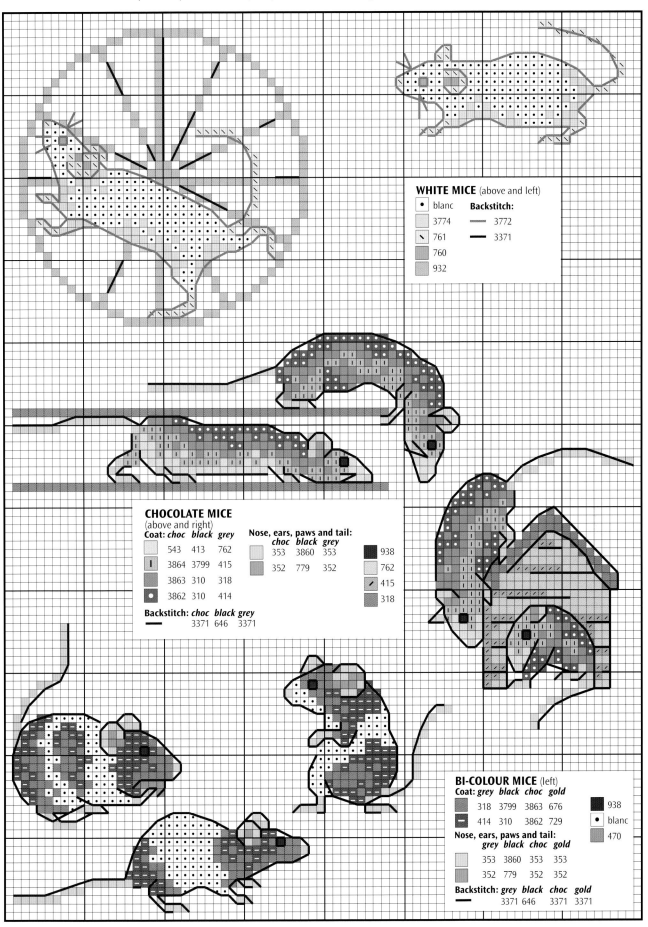

WHITE MICE (above and left)

		Backstitch:	
•	blanc		
	3774	—	3772
\	761	—	3371
	760		
	932		

CHOCOLATE MICE
(above and right)

Coat:	*choc*	*black*	*grey*
	543	413	762
I	3864	3799	415
	3863	310	318
•	3862	310	414

Nose, ears, paws and tail:

	choc	*black*	*grey*
	353	3860	353
	352	779	352

	938
	762
✔	415
	318

Backstitch:	*choc*	*black*	*grey*
—	3371	646	3371

BI-COLOUR MICE (left)

Coat:	*grey*	*black*	*choc*	*gold*
	318	3799	3863	676
—	414	310	3862	729

Nose, ears, paws and tail:

	grey	*black*	*choc*	*gold*
	353	3860	353	353
	352	779	352	352

	938
•	blanc
	470

Backstitch:	*grey*	*black*	*choc*	*gold*
—	3371	646	3371	3371

Ferrets are intelligent, curious and friendly, and can be trained to go for a walk on the end of a lead.

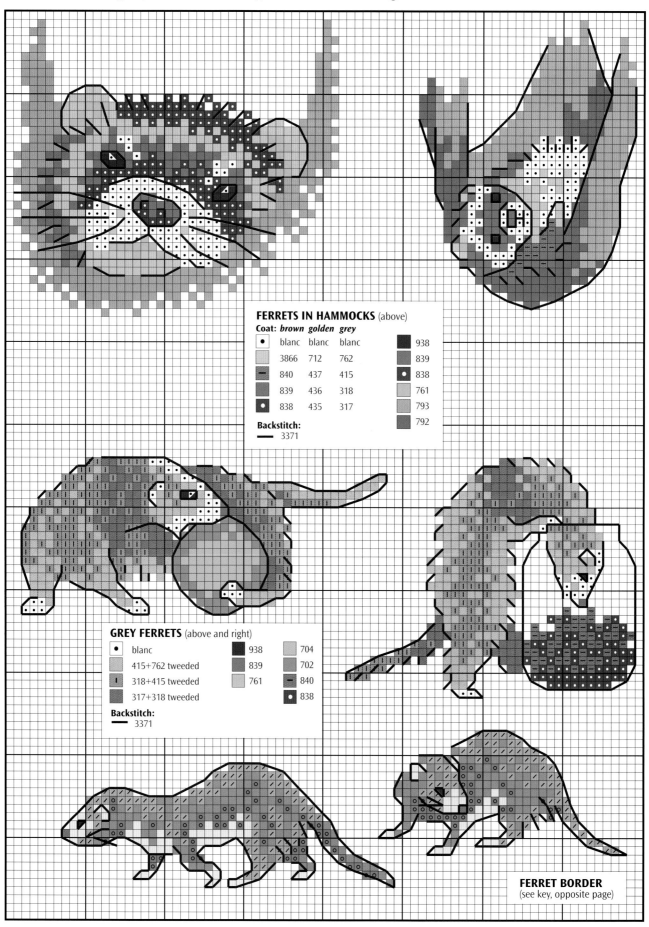

FERRETS IN HAMMOCKS (above)

Coat:	*brown*	*golden*	*grey*		
•	blanc	blanc	blanc		938
	3866	712	762		839
–	840	437	415		838
	839	436	318		761
⊙	838	435	317		793
					792

Backstitch:
— 3371

GREY FERRETS (above and right)

•	blanc		938		704
	415+762 tweeded		839		702
I	318+415 tweeded		761	–	840
	317+318 tweeded			⊙	838

Backstitch:
— 3371

FERRET BORDER
(see key, opposite page)

Ferrets will burrow into anything, often hiding in your socks, your clothes, cupboards and boxes.

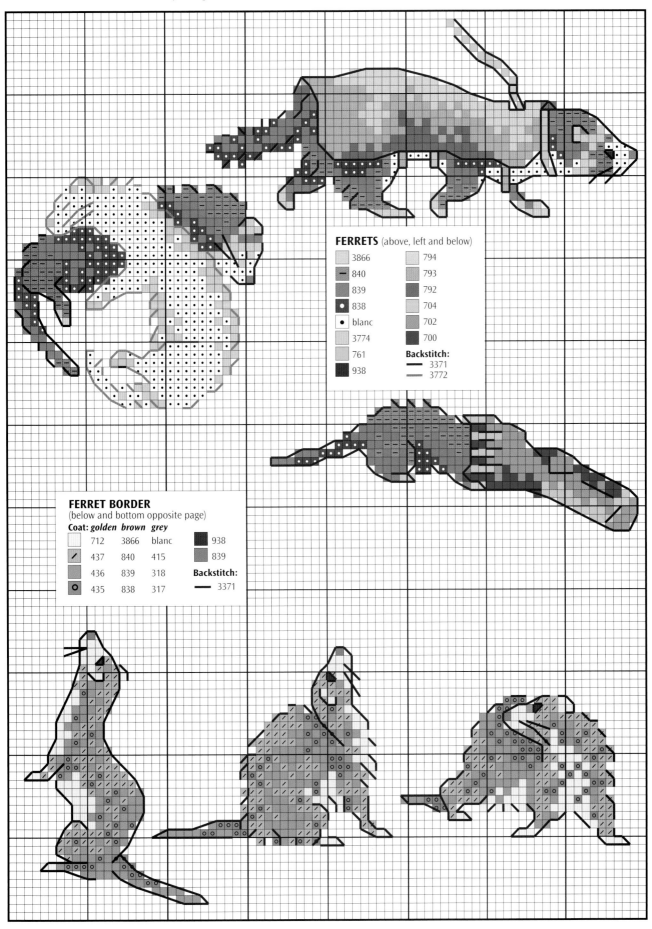

FERRETS (above, left and below)

3866		794	
— 840		793	
839		792	
838		704	
• blanc		702	
3774		700	
761		**Backstitch:**	
938		— 3371	
		— 3772	

FERRET BORDER
(below and bottom opposite page)
Coat: *golden brown grey*

	golden	brown	grey
	712	3866	blanc
╱	437	840	415
	436	839	318
⊙	435	838	317

938	
839	
Backstitch:	
— 3371	

SCALES &
FEATHERS

This chapter covers a range of fascinating pets. Birds are high on glamour, with attractive plumage, beautiful songs and distinct personalities. Fish are fascinating and their stunning colours and interesting movements can be very relaxing. Reptiles are popular because of their exotic colours, patterns and textures and can be calming. They are other-worldly, like prehistoric creatures and miniature dragons. The charts start with birds, including pretty budgies, finches, canaries and colourful parrots and cockatoos. Then there are goldfish and tropical fish. Reptiles are next – from the sedate tortoise and chameleon to speedier geckos, followed by a stunning green iguana and boa constrictors. Pets with scales and feathers make attractive cross stitch designs and suit smaller projects, such as the bookmark and key ring shown here. The designs can also be grouped to decorate larger items, like a diary and washbag.

Keep a diary of your pet's activities, adding photos and useful care information. Here, a patch of two playful geckos (page 87) is stitched on 14-count white Aida using two strands of stranded cotton (floss) for cross stitch and one for backstitch. The patch was then backed with iron-on interfacing (see page 100) and stuck on a notebook using double-sided adhesive tape.

You could stitch your own pet and add a label stitched using one of the alphabets in the book. The green iguana (page 87) would make a very impressive book cover for a school project.

Stitch count: 33 x 54.
Design size: 6 x 9.8cm (2⅜ x 3½in) on 14-count.

A bookmark displays a multicoloured scarlet macaw (page 82) beautifully. It is stitched on 14-count white Aida using two strands of stranded cotton (floss) for cross stitch and one for backstitch. Make up the bookmark according to the instructions on page 103 – the finished bookmark is 20 x 7cm (8 x 2¾in). Add a ready-made tassel or make your own by using leftover threads (see page 100).

Work your own favourite motif instead – perhaps a vertical row of pretty finches (page 81) or three goldfish (page 84).

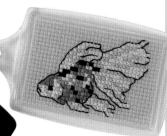

Stitch count: 58 x 28.
Design size: 10.5 x 5cm (4⅛ x 2in) on 14-count.

This little sign is the perfect reminder to lock the door of this green boa constrictor's (page 86) tank! It is stitched on 14-count white Aida using two strands of stranded cotton (floss) for cross stitch and one for backstitch. The words are worked using the alphabet on page 42 in DMC 905. When the stitching is completed, make up according to the instructions on page 102. The finished sign is 12.5cm (5in) square.

You could make other signs to remind you when to feed your pet, or take it for a walk, or to prepare others that may be startled coming face to face with a snake!

Stitch count: 58 x 37.
Design size: 10.5 x 6.7cm (4⅛ x 1½in) on 14-count.

A key ring is great for mounting small motifs. This elegant Veiltail goldfish (page 84) is stitched on 14-count light blue Aida using two strands of stranded cotton (floss) for cross stitch and one for backstitch. Back the stitching with iron-on interfacing (see page 100) and mount into the key ring according to the manufacturer's instructions. This key ring aperture is 4.5 x 6.3cm (1¾ x 2½in).

If using another motif, make sure that it will fit into the key ring (see calculating design size page 98). Alternatively, the goldfish and tropical fish designs would be perfect for a collection of coasters or paperweights.

Stitch count: 21 x 29.
Design size: 3.8 x 5cm (1½ x 2in) on 14-count.

A ready-made washbag features a colourful shoal of tropical fish (page 85). They are stitched over two fabric threads of 28-count light blue evenweave using two strands of stranded cotton (floss) for cross stitch and one for backstitch. Bubbles linking the fish are worked in DMC 996. The patch is 17 x 15.2cm (6¾ x 6in) and is backed with iron-on interfacing (see page 100). It is then stitched to the bag front, carefully to avoid puncturing the waterproof liner. The washbag is 25.5 x 21.5cm (10 x 8½in).

Stitch a single fish, or make up your own shoal of goldfish or tropical fish. Plan it on graph paper first (see page 98) to make sure that it will fit on to the bag.

Stitch count: 81 x 76.
Design size: 14.7 x 13.8cm (5¾ x 5½in) on 28-count.

A widely kept bird, budgerigars make good companions and will happily chirp, trill and whistle to their owners.

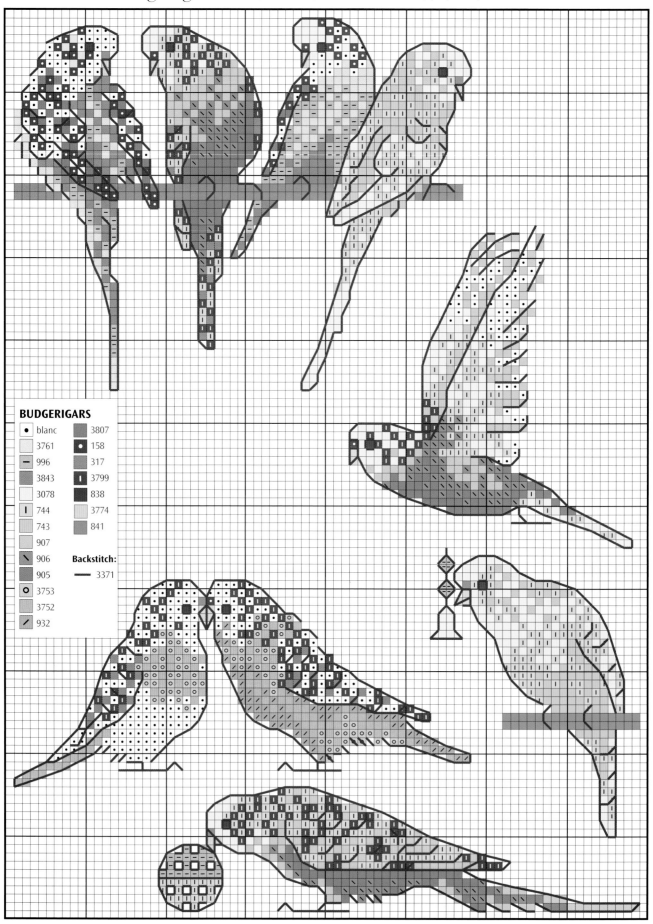

BUDGERIGARS

●	blanc		3807
	3761	●	158
—	996		317
	3843	I	3799
	3078		838
I	744		3774
	743		841
	907		
\	906	**Backstitch:**	
	905	—	3371
O	3753		
	3752		
/	932		

Finches need a large aviary to spread their wings. Some canaries are bred for looks, some for singing.

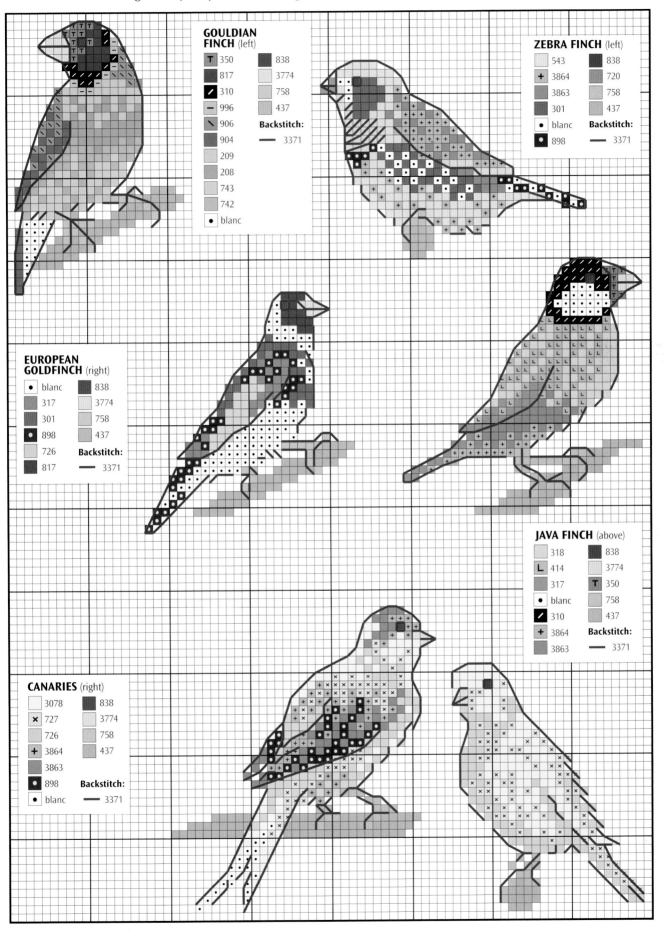

GOULDIAN FINCH (left)

T	350		838
	817		3774
/	310		758
−	996		437
\	906		
	904		
	209		
	208		
	743		
	742		
•	blanc		

Backstitch:
— 3371

ZEBRA FINCH (left)

	543		838
+	3864		720
	3863		758
	301		437
•	blanc		
⊡	898		

Backstitch:
— 3371

EUROPEAN GOLDFINCH (right)

•	blanc		838
	317		3774
	301		758
⊡	898		437
	726		
	817		

Backstitch:
— 3371

JAVA FINCH (above)

	318		838
L	414		3774
	317	T	350
•	blanc		758
/	310		437
+	3864		
	3863		

Backstitch:
— 3371

CANARIES (right)

	3078		838
×	727		3774
	726		758
+	3864		437
	3863		
⊡	898		
•	blanc		

Backstitch:
— 3371

Parrots are good talkers, particularly the African grey parrot, and may repeat things you wish they wouldn't!

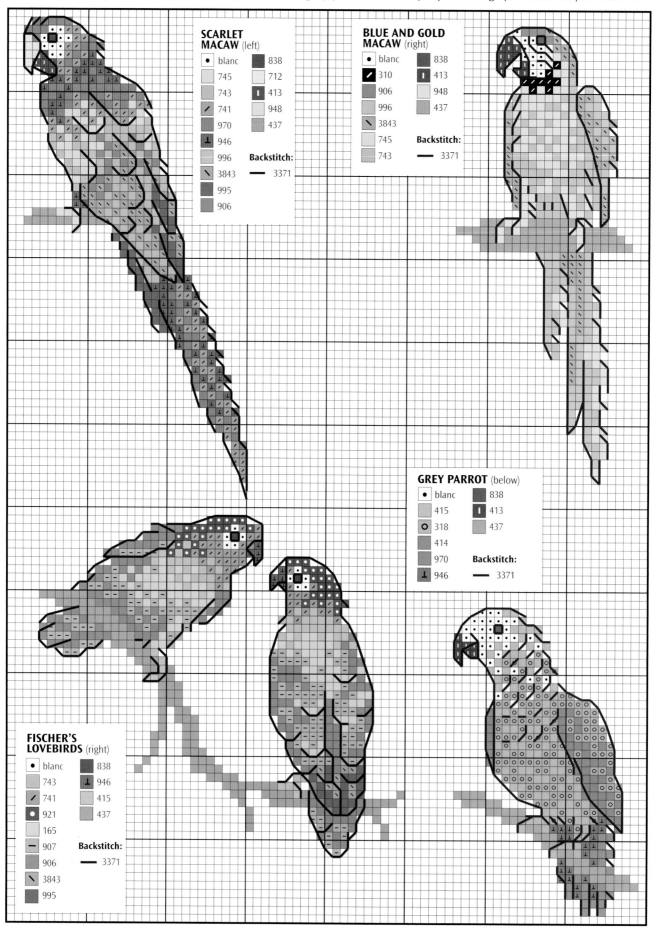

SCARLET MACAW (left)

• blanc	■ 838
745	712
743	I 413
╱ 741	948
970	437
⊥ 946	
996	**Backstitch:**
╲ 3843	— 3371
995	
906	

BLUE AND GOLD MACAW (right)

• blanc	■ 838
╱ 310	I 413
906	948
996	437
╲ 3843	
745	**Backstitch:**
743	— 3371

GREY PARROT (below)

• blanc	■ 838
415	I 413
⊙ 318	437
414	
970	**Backstitch:**
⊥ 946	— 3371

FISCHER'S LOVEBIRDS (right)

• blanc	■ 838
743	⊥ 946
╱ 741	415
⊙ 921	437
165	
— 907	**Backstitch:**
906	— 3371
╲ 3843	
995	

Cockatoos, lovebirds and parrots become very attached to their human families and can be very long lived.

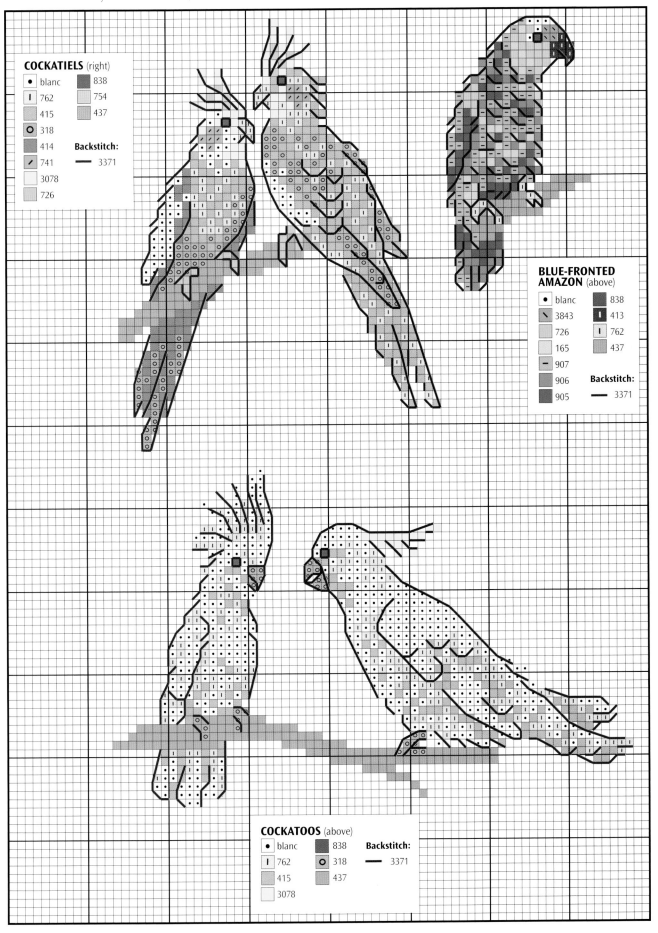

COCKATIELS (right)

• blanc	838
I 762	754
415	437
O 318	
414	**Backstitch:**
/ 741	— 3371
3078	
726	

BLUE-FRONTED AMAZON (above)

• blanc	838
\ 3843	I 413
726	I 762
165	437
— 907	
906	**Backstitch:**
905	— 3371

COCKATOOS (above)

• blanc	838	**Backstitch:**
I 762	O 318	— 3371
415	437	
3078		

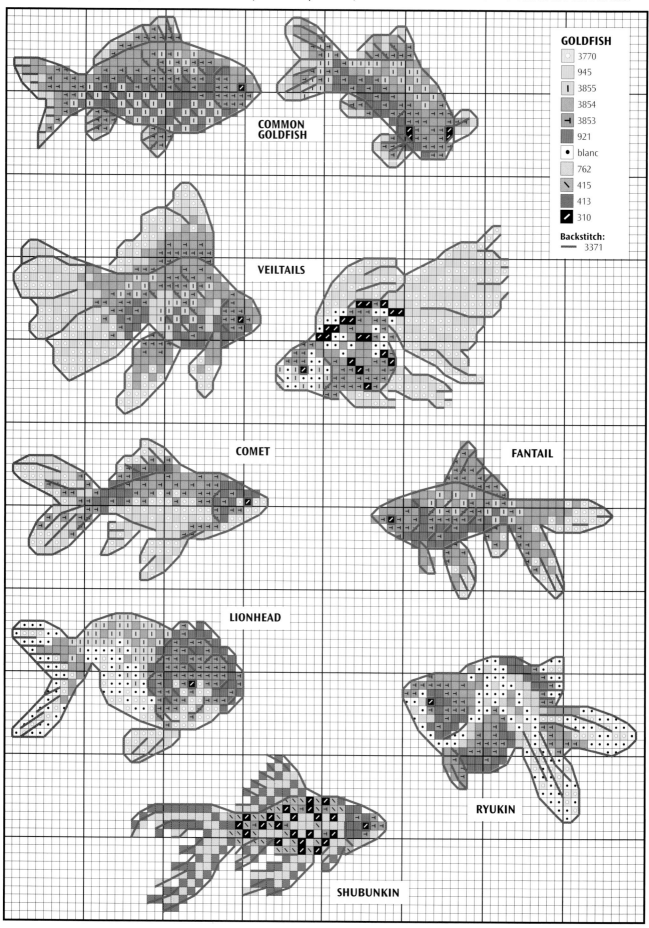

COMMON GOLDFISH

VEILTAILS

COMET

FANTAIL

LIONHEAD

RYUKIN

SHUBUNKIN

GOLDFISH	
○	3770
	945
I	3855
	3854
⊢	3853
	921
•	blanc
	762
\	415
	413
◤	310

Backstitch:
— 3371

Tropical fish, whether marine or freshwater, are flamboyantly colourful and can be unusual shapes too.

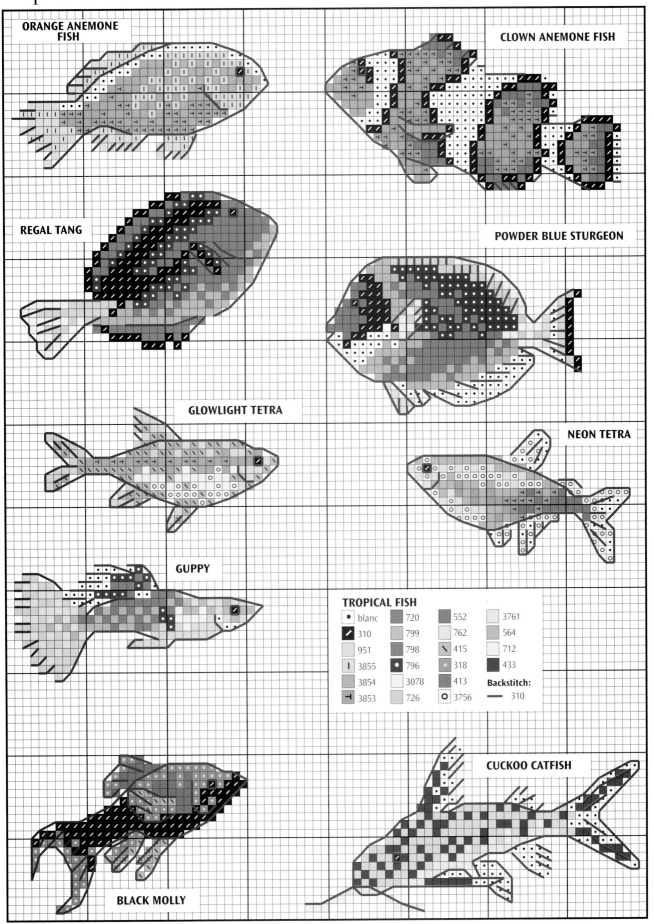

ORANGE ANEMONE FISH

CLOWN ANEMONE FISH

REGAL TANG

POWDER BLUE STURGEON

GLOWLIGHT TETRA

NEON TETRA

GUPPY

TROPICAL FISH

• blanc	720	552	3761
310	799	762	564
951	798	415	712
3855	796	318	433
3854	3078	413	Backstitch:
3853	726	O 3756	— 310

CUCKOO CATFISH

BLACK MOLLY

Snakes, geckos and tortoises make fascinating pets, though boas need more experienced owners.

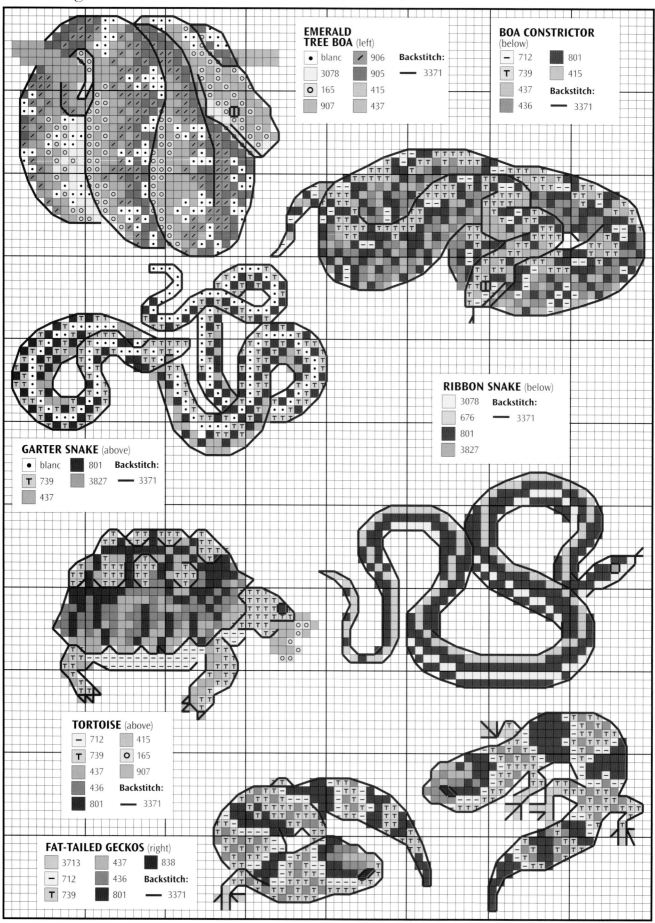

EMERALD TREE BOA (left)

• blanc	/ 906	**Backstitch:**		
3078	905	— 3371		
O 165	415			
907	437			

BOA CONSTRICTOR (below)

— 712	801	
T 739	415	
437	**Backstitch:**	
436	— 3371	

RIBBON SNAKE (below)

3078	**Backstitch:**
676	— 3371
801	
3827	

GARTER SNAKE (above)

• blanc	801	**Backstitch:**
T 739	3827	— 3371
437		

TORTOISE (above)

— 712	415
T 739	O 165
437	907
436	**Backstitch:**
801	— 3371

FAT-TAILED GECKOS (right)

3713	437	838
— 712	436	**Backstitch:**
T 739	801	— 3371

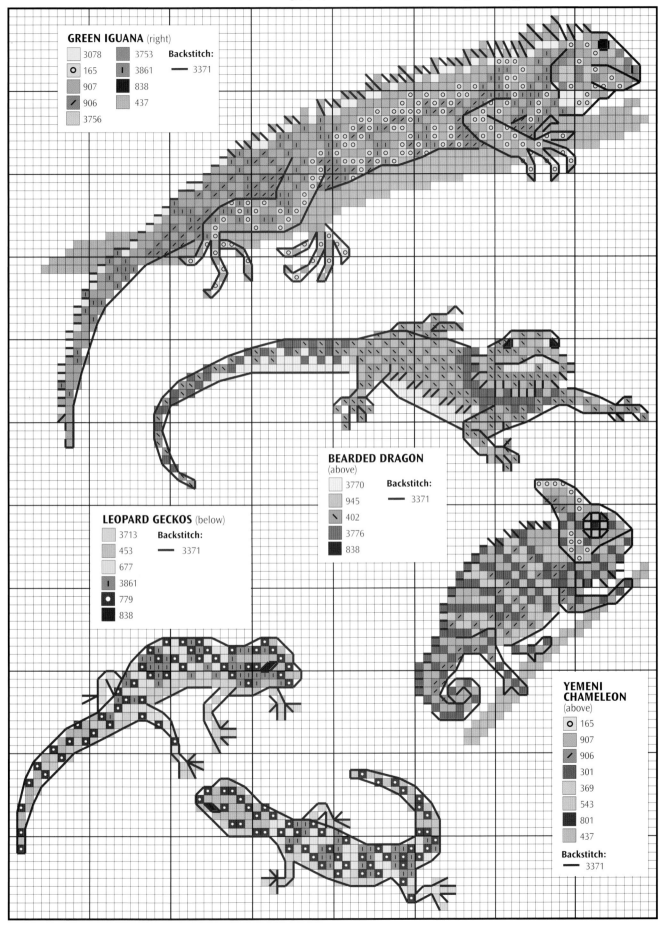

GREEN IGUANA (right)

				Backstitch:
	3078		3753	
○	165	I	3861	— 3371
	907		838	
╱	906		437	
	3756			

BEARDED DRAGON
(above)

		Backstitch:
	3770	
	945	— 3371
╱	402	
	3776	
	838	

LEOPARD GECKOS (below)

		Backstitch:
	3713	
	453	— 3371
	677	
I	3861	
●	779	
	838	

YEMENI CHAMELEON
(above)

○	165
	907
╱	906
	301
	369
	543
	801
	437

Backstitch:
— 3371

HORSES
& FARMYARD FRIENDS

This chapter is devoted to larger animals that often work for a living. Horses will take you riding, help with ranch or farm work and join you in competitions. You must get up early to feed, muck out, exercise, groom and clean tack, but a well-cared for horse will reward you with loyalty, friendship and an eagerness to join you in rides and competitions. The many joys of horses and ponies are depicted in six pages of charts, featuring the most popular breeds. Horse lovers will have great fun using the designs, as the picture opposite shows. Farmyard friends aren't forgotten either as they often become pets and companions. There are charming charts of chickens, geese and ducks – see the Welcome Sampler on page 5 for ideas on using these motifs. There are also charts for pampered pigs, sheep and goats.

This delightful picture

shows dressage, show jumping and cross country events (page 92) stitched on 14-count cream Aida using two strands of stranded cotton (floss) for cross stitch and one for backstitch. Mark the vertical centre line on the Aida with tacking (basting) stitches and stitch each motif centrally on this line with four rows of Aida separating each. Frame your picture referring to page 102. This frame aperture is 13.3 x 28cm (5¼ x 11in).

Stitch count: 129 x 52.
Design size: 23.4 x 9.5cm (9¼ x 3¾in) on 14-count.

Customize a rosette with a

portrait of your horse (page 93) by stitching it on 16-count white Aida using two strands of stranded cotton (floss) for cross stitch and one for backstitch. To cover the back of the stitching, cut a circle of iron-on interfacing and carefully iron it into place (see page 100). Use double-sided adhesive tape to stick the embroidery to a ready-made rosette. This rosette has a centre diameter of 8.5cm (3¼in).

Stitch count: 51 x 39.
Design size: 8 x 6.2cm (3⅛ x 2½in) on 16-count.

A photo album is perfect for

displaying the excitement of pony club games (page 95). The patch is stitched on 14-count cream Aida using two strands of stranded cotton (floss) for cross stitch and one for backstitch. Use the alphabet on page 42 to personalize the design using DMC 987. When stitching is completed, back the patch with iron-on interfacing (see page 100) and cut to size to fit your album, sticking in place with double-sided tape.

Stitch count: 61 x 44.
Design size: 11 x 8cm (4⅜ x 3⅛in) on 14-count.

Instead of sticking cross stitched patches on a rosette or book cover, you could create a patch for a garment, such as a sweatshirt or jacket, hemming the edges befire sewing the patch on.

The five most **popular horse breeds** are Thoroughbred, American Paint, American Quarter, Arab and Appaloosa.

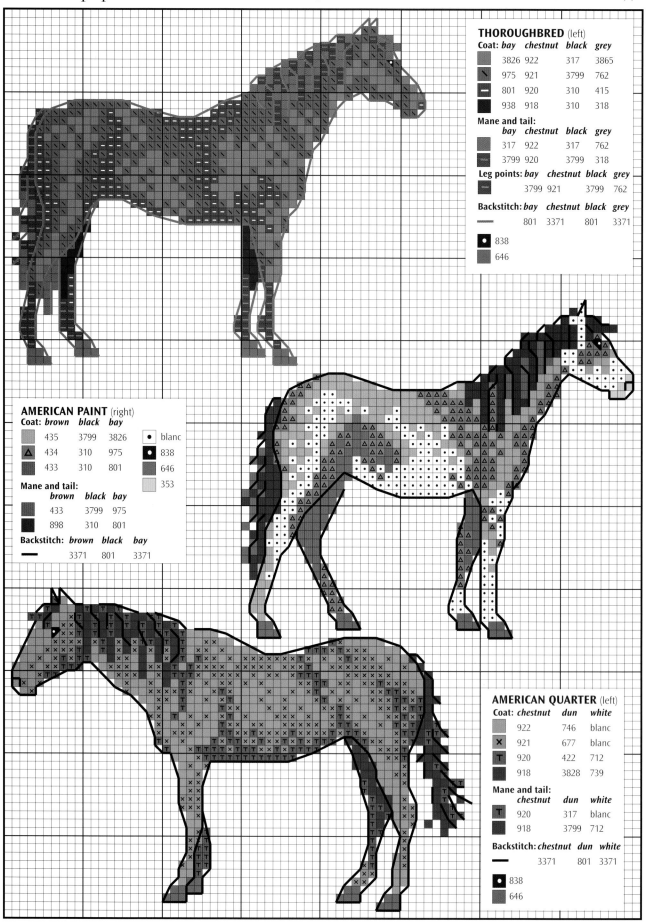

THOROUGHBRED (left)

Coat:	bay	chestnut	black	grey
	3826	922	317	3865
	975	921	3799	762
	801	920	310	415
	938	918	310	318

Mane and tail:

	bay	chestnut	black	grey
	317	922	317	762
	3799	920	3799	318

Leg points:	bay	chestnut	black	grey
	3799	921	3799	762

Backstitch:	bay	chestnut	black	grey
	801	3371	801	3371

•	838
	646

AMERICAN PAINT (right)

Coat:	brown	black	bay		
	435	3799	3826	•	blanc
△	434	310	975	⦿	838
	433	310	801		646
					353

Mane and tail:

	brown	black	bay
	433	3799	975
	898	310	801

Backstitch:	brown	black	bay
—	3371	801	3371

AMERICAN QUARTER (left)

Coat:	chestnut	dun	white
	922	746	blanc
×	921	677	blanc
T	920	422	712
	918	3828	739

Mane and tail:

	chestnut	dun	white
T	920	317	blanc
	918	3799	712

Backstitch:	chestnut	dun	white
—	3371	801	3371

⦿	838
	646

The Arab has speed, stamina and agility. The Appaloosa has six types of markings, including frost and snowflake.

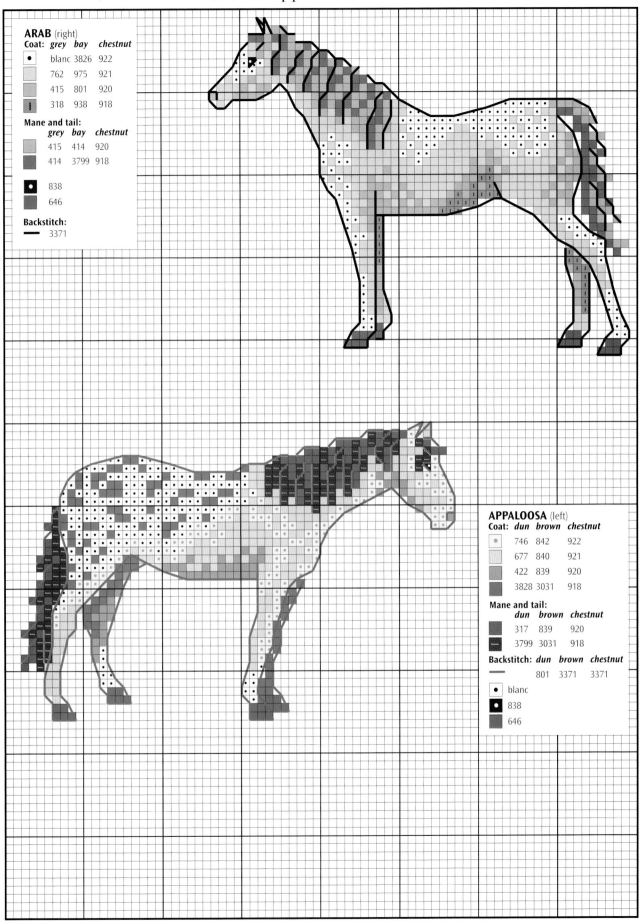

ARAB (right)
Coat:

	grey	bay	chestnut
•	blanc	3826	922
	762	975	921
	415	801	920
∎	318	938	918

Mane and tail:

	grey	bay	chestnut
	415	414	920
	414	3799	918
⊙	838		
	646		

Backstitch:

—	3371

APPALOOSA (left)
Coat:

	dun	brown	chestnut
•	746	842	922
	677	840	921
	422	839	920
	3828	3031	918

Mane and tail:

	dun	brown	chestnut
	317	839	920
	3799	3031	918

Backstitch:

	dun	brown	chestnut
—		801	3371	3371
•	blanc		
⊙	838		
	646		

Competition horses take part in the equestrian sports of show jumping, dressage and eventing.

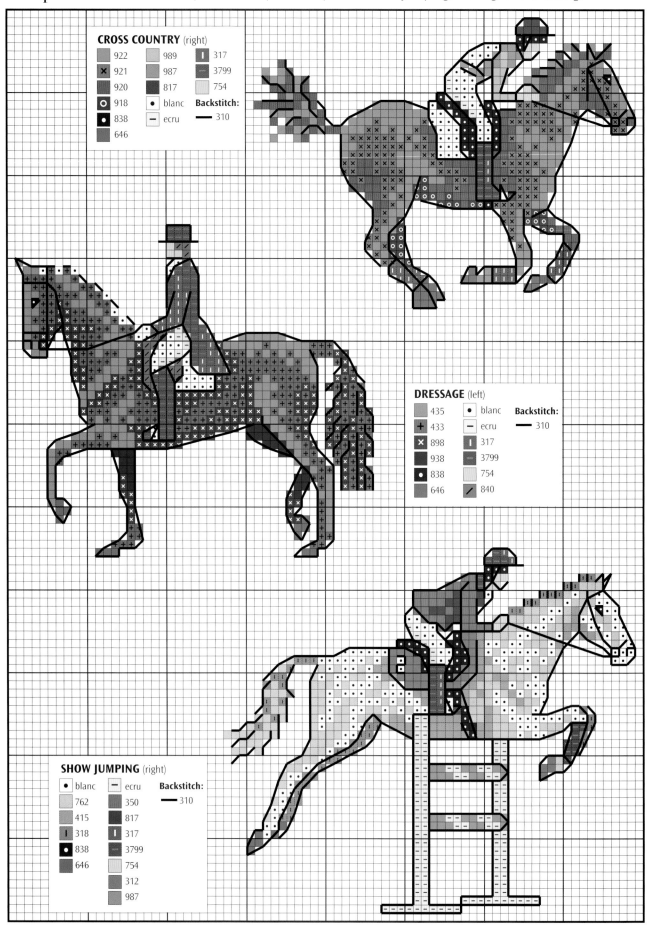

CROSS COUNTRY (right)

▨	922	▨	989	I	317	
×	921	▨	987	▨	3799	
▨	920	▨	817	▨	754	
⊙	918	•	blanc	**Backstitch:**	
◖	838	−	ecru	— 310	
▨	646				

DRESSAGE (left)

▨	435	•	blanc	**Backstitch:**
+	433	−	ecru	— 310
×	898	I	317	
▨	938	▨	3799	
◖	838	▨	754	
▨	646	╱	840	

SHOW JUMPING (right)

•	blanc	−	ecru	**Backstitch:**
▨	762	▨	350	— 310
▨	415	▨	817	
I	318	I	317	
◖	838	▨	3799	
▨	646	▨	754	
		▨	312	
		▨	987	

The horse has four natural ways of walking or gaits – walk, trot, canter and gallop.

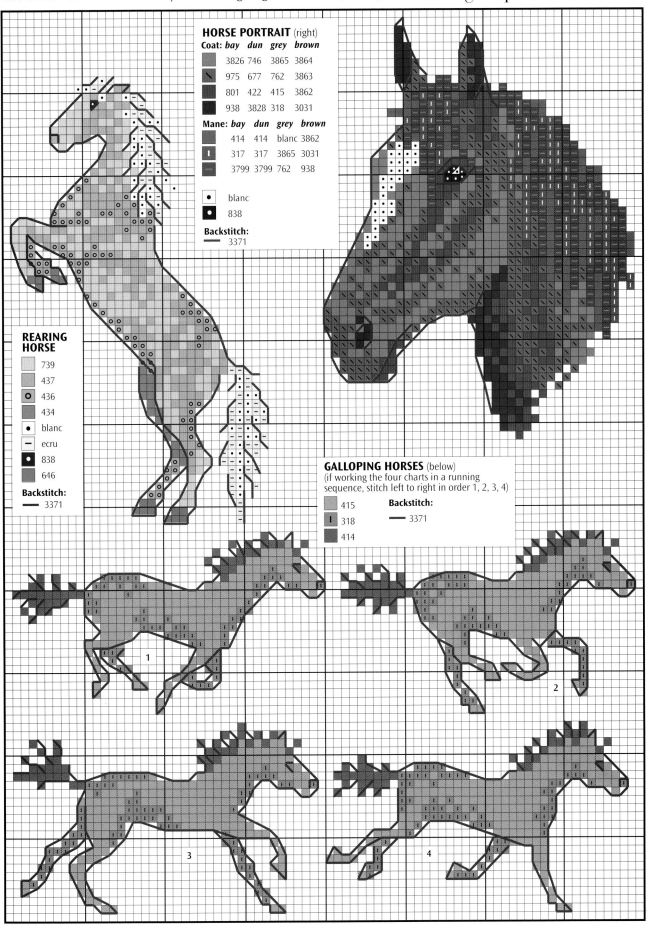

HORSE PORTRAIT (right)

Coat:	*bay*	*dun*	*grey*	*brown*
	3826	746	3865	3864
	975	677	762	3863
	801	422	415	3862
	938	3828	318	3031

Mane:	*bay*	*dun*	*grey*	*brown*
	414	414	blanc	3862
	317	317	3865	3031
	3799	3799	762	938

• blanc
⊙ 838

Backstitch:
— 3371

REARING HORSE

- 739
- 437
- ⊙ 436
- 434
- • blanc
- – ecru
- ⊙ 838
- 646

Backstitch:
— 3371

GALLOPING HORSES (below)
(if working the four charts in a running sequence, stitch left to right in order 1, 2, 3, 4)

- 415
- I 318
- 414

Backstitch:
— 3371

1

2

3

4

Many pony breeds are natives to moors, mountains and forests and are sturdy, strong and sure-footed.

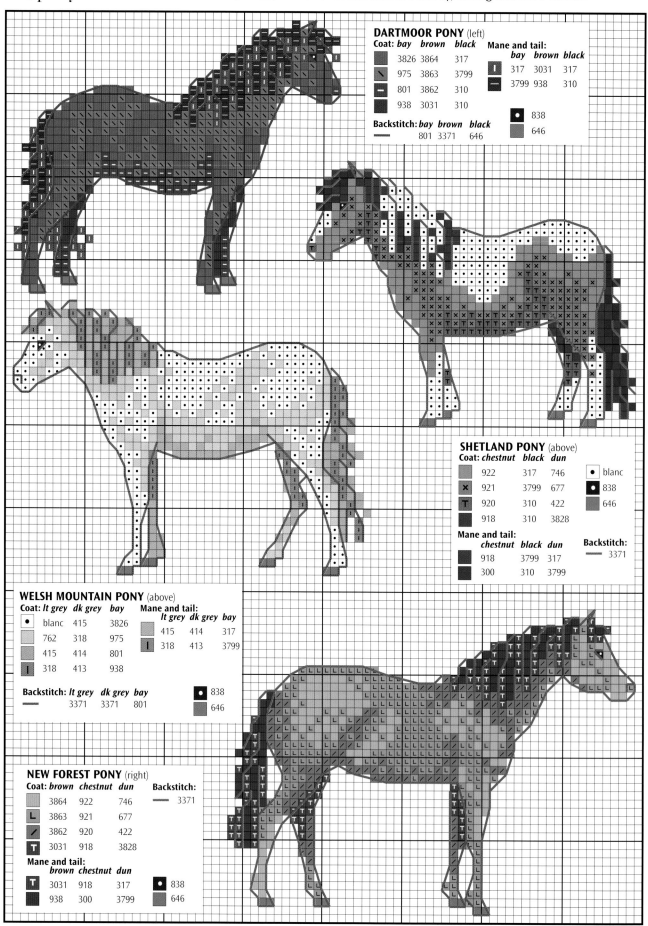

DARTMOOR PONY (left)

Coat:	*bay*	*brown*	*black*
	3826	3864	317
\	975	3863	3799
−	801	3862	310
	938	3031	310

Mane and tail:	*bay*	*brown*	*black*
I	317	3031	317
−	3799	938	310

	838
	646

Backstitch:	*bay*	*brown*	*black*
—	801	3371	646

SHETLAND PONY (above)

Coat:	*chestnut*	*black*	*dun*
	922	317	746
×	921	3799	677
T	920	310	422
	918	310	3828

Mane and tail:	*chestnut*	*black*	*dun*
	918	3799	317
	300	310	3799

•	blanc
	838
	646

Backstitch:
— 3371

WELSH MOUNTAIN PONY (above)

Coat:	*lt grey*	*dk grey*	*bay*
•	blanc	415	3826
	762	318	975
	415	414	801
I	318	413	938

Mane and tail:	*lt grey*	*dk grey*	*bay*
	415	414	317
I	318	413	3799

Backstitch:	*lt grey*	*dk grey*	*bay*
—	3371	3371	801

	838
	646

NEW FOREST PONY (right)

Coat:	*brown*	*chestnut*	*dun*
	3864	922	746
L	3863	921	677
/	3862	920	422
T	3031	918	3828

Backstitch:
— 3371

Mane and tail:	*brown*	*chestnut*	*dun*
T	3031	918	317
	938	300	3799

	838
	646

94 HORSES & FARMYARD FRIENDS

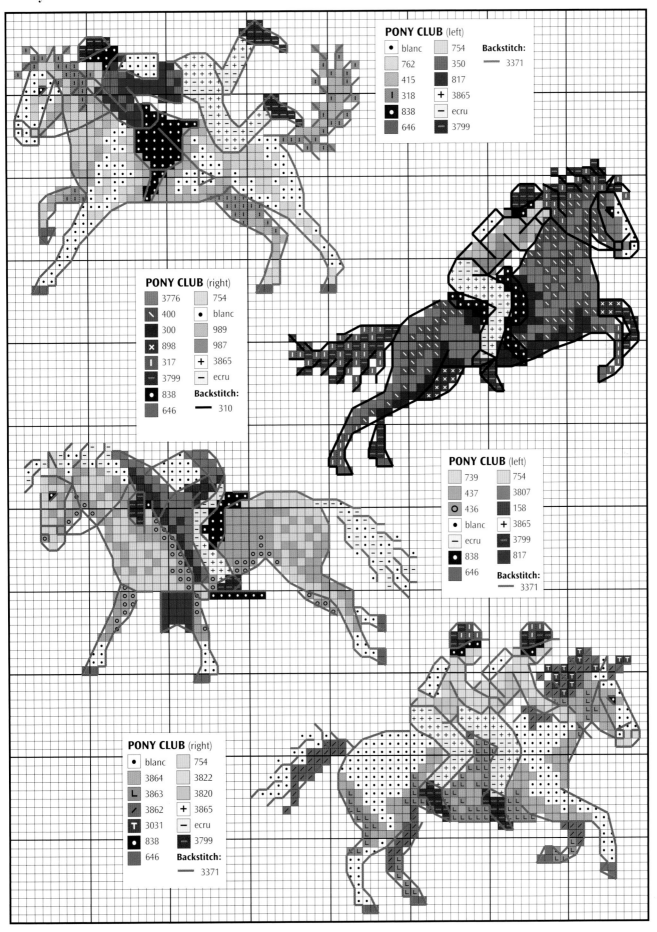

PONY CLUB (left)

•	blanc		754
	762		350
	415		817
I	318	+	3865
●	838	—	ecru
	646		3799

Backstitch:
— 3371

PONY CLUB (right)

	3776		754
╲	400	•	blanc
	300		989
✕	898		987
I	317	+	3865
	3799	—	ecru
●	838		
	646	Backstitch:	
		—	310

PONY CLUB (left)

	739		754
	437		3807
O	436		158
•	blanc	+	3865
—	ecru		3799
●	838		817
	646	Backstitch:	
		—	3371

PONY CLUB (right)

•	blanc		754
	3864		3822
L	3863		3820
╱	3862	+	3865
T	3031	—	ecru
●	838		3799
	646	Backstitch:	
		—	3371

Geese make good 'watch dogs', chickens enjoy suburban gardens and ducks will set up home in any pond.

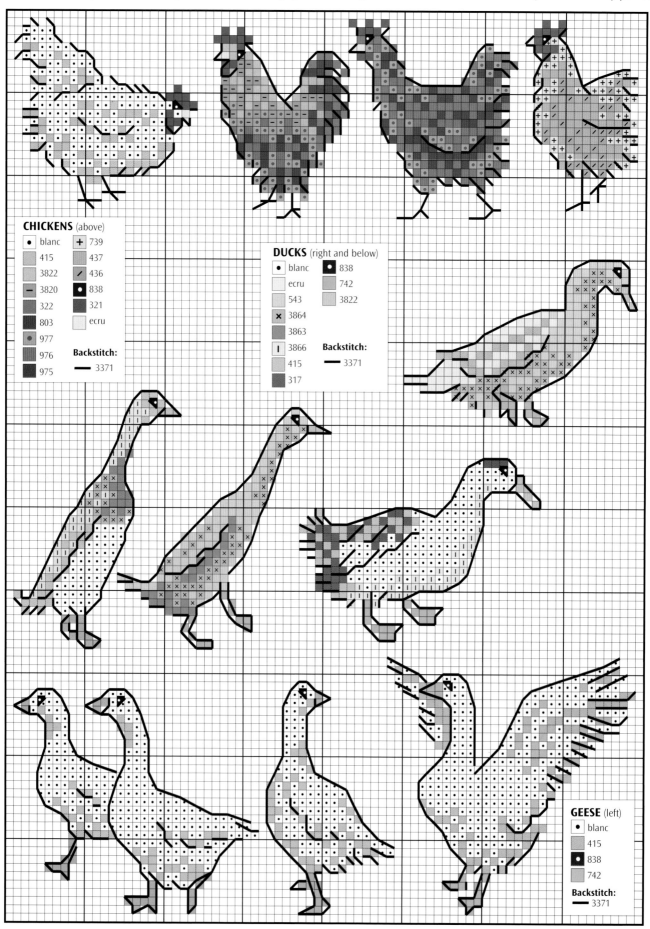

CHICKENS (above)
- blanc
- 415
- 3822
- 3820
- 322
- 803
- 977
- 976
- 975
- 739
- 437
- 436
- 838
- 321
- ecru

Backstitch:
— 3371

DUCKS (right and below)
- blanc
- ecru
- 543
- 3864
- 3863
- 3866
- 415
- 317
- 838
- 742
- 3822

Backstitch:
— 3371

GEESE (left)
- blanc
- 415
- 838
- 742

Backstitch:
— 3371

Today, many farm animals such as goats, sheep and pigs are kept as pets and become part of the family.

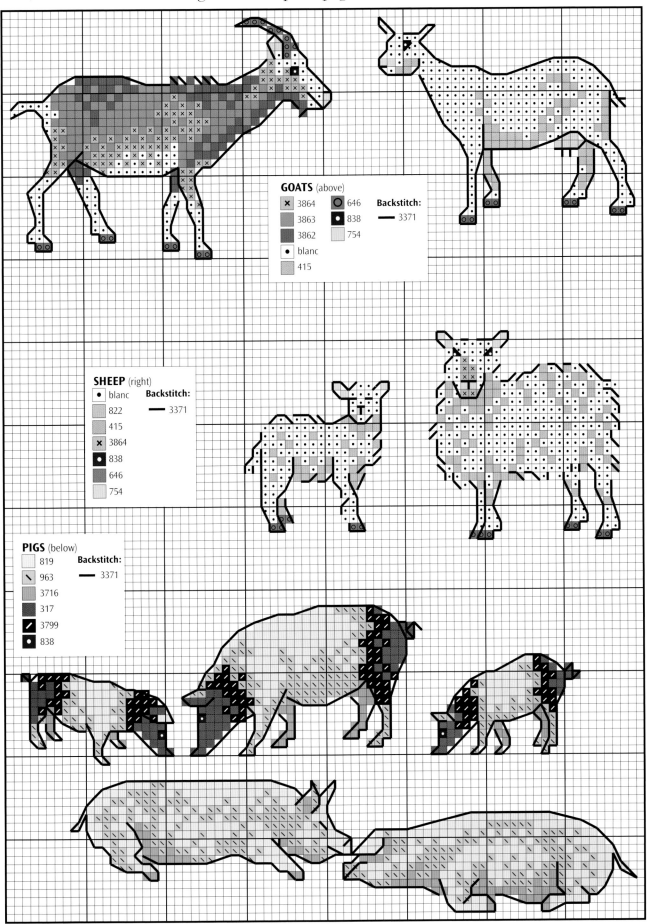

GOATS (above)

					Backstitch:
✕	3864	◯	646		—— 3371
	3863	●	838		
	3862		754		
●	blanc				
	415				

SHEEP (right)

		Backstitch:
●	blanc	—— 3371
	822	
	415	
✕	3864	
●	838	
	646	
	754	

PIGS (below)

		Backstitch:
	819	—— 3371
╲	963	
	3716	
	317	
╱	3799	
●	838	

MATERIALS AND TECHNIQUES

This section describes the materials and equipment required for cross stitch embroidery and the basic stitching techniques used.

Materials

Very few materials are required for the cross stitch in this book, although you can of course customize your work.

Fabrics

The designs have mostly been worked on Aida fabric where one block corresponds to one square on the chart and one cross stitch is made over one block using the holes as a guide. The designs could also be stitched on an evenweave such as linen but you will need to work over two fabric threads, to even out any oddities in the thread thicknesses. A design worked on 14-count Aida will be the same size if stitched on 28-count evenweave.

Threads

The projects have been stitched with DMC stranded embroidery cotton (floss) but you could match the colours to other thread ranges. Some metallic threads have also been used. The six-stranded skeins can easily be split into separate strands. The various project instructions tell you how many strands to use.

You can create more colours by tweeding threads, that is combining two colours in the needle at the same time and working as one to create a mottled effect. The two colours will be listed together in the key. For example, 436 + 3031 means using one strand of 436 together with one strand of 3031.

Needles

Tapestry needles are used for cross stitch as they have a round point and do not snag fabric. Sizes 24–26 are the most common.

Frames

Whether you use an embroidery frame to keep your fabric taut while stitching is a matter of personal preference. Working with a frame helps to keep the tension even and prevent distortion, while working without a frame is faster and less cumbersome. There are various types on the market – look in your local needlework shop.

Techniques

Your cross stitch embroidery will look its best if you follow the simple guidelines below.

Preparing the Fabric

Before starting work, check the design size given with each project and make sure that this agrees with the size you require for your finished embroidery – see below for calculating design size. Cut your fabric at least 7.5cm (3in) larger all the way round than the finished size of the stitching to allow for making up, and at least 15cm (6in) larger all round if the design is to be framed. Before you begin stitching, carefully neaten the edges of the fabric by hemming to stop it fraying.

Finding the Fabric Centre

Marking the centre of the fabric is important in order to stitch the design centrally on the fabric. To find the centre, fold the fabric in half horizontally and then vertically, then tack (baste) along the folds (or use tailor's chalk). The centre point is where the two lines cross. This point on the fabric should correspond to the centre point on the chart. Remove the lines on completion of the work.

Calculating Design Size

Each project gives the stitch count and finished design size but if you want to work the design on a different count fabric or to check you are working on a large enough piece of fabric you will need to re-calculate the finished size, as follows.

Count the number of stitches across the whole design at the widest point and also along the height of the design. Now divide each of these numbers by the count of the fabric that you want to use and this will give you the finished design size.

For example, if a motif is 56 stitches wide and 49 stitches high, the finished design size on a 14-count fabric will be 4 x 3½in (10 x 9cm). On a 16-count fabric it will be 3½ x 3in (9 x 7.6cm). Working on evenweave usually means working over two threads, so divide the fabric count by two before you start calculating.

Once you know the finished size, measure the aperture or size of the item you want to display your embroidery in and compare the two. If the motif is too big to fit when worked on 14-count fabric, it may fit if worked on 16-count as the finished size will be smaller. Always allow a small margin of fabric between the motif and the aperture so the motif doesn't look forced into the space.

Using Charts and Keys

The charts in this book are easy to work from. Each square on the chart represents one stitch. Each coloured square, or coloured square with a symbol, represents a thread colour, with the code number given in the chart key. An empty square represents unworked fabric. A few of the designs use fractional stitches (three-quarter cross stitches) to give more definition to the design. These are represented by a coloured triangle rather than a full square. Solid coloured lines show where backstitches are to be worked. Most chart pages have several keys that are labelled to show you which charted motifs they are used for. See page 6 for using the chart keys when working different coat colours.

Washing and Pressing

If it is necessary to wash your embroidery, use warm water and a non-biological powder or liquid. Rinse well and roll the stitching in a towel to blot off the water. Never wring your stitching.

It is easier to iron your stitching while it is still damp, and this will also dry it. To iron your work, use a medium setting and cover the ironing board with a thick layer of towelling. Place the stitching right side down and press gently.

Working the Stitches

Only three basic stitches have been used for the projects in this book, all described here.

Starting and Finishing Stitching

It is best to start and finish work neatly in order to avoid a lumpy, uneven look when your work is mounted.

Use a knotless loop start (Fig 1) if working with an even number of strands i.e. 2, 4 or 6. To start with two strands cut the stranded cotton (floss) twice the length that you would normally use. Separate one strand, fold it in half and thread a needle with the two ends. From the wrong side, push the needle up through the fabric where the first stitch is to be, leaving the loop hanging at the back. Form a half cross stitch and pass the needle through the waiting loop. Pull tight and the thread is now anchored. If using four strands, cut two strands of cotton (floss) and fold in half.

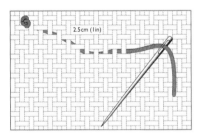

Fig 1
Knotless loop start

Use an away waste knot start (Fig 2) if working with an odd number of strands or a tweeded thread. Thread your needle and knot the end. From the front, push the needle down through the fabric about 2.5cm (1in) away from where you want the first stitch to be. Begin the first stitch and work over this thread until it is firmly anchored. Cut off the knot and trim any excess thread neatly.

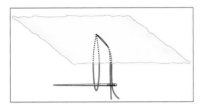

Fig 2
Away waste knot start

To finish off thread, pass the needle through some nearby stitches on the wrong side of the work, then cut the thread off close to the fabric. You can also start a new thread in a similar way.

Backstitch

This gives definition and outlines areas of a design. Some charts use different coloured backstitches and the colour may change if you stitch your pet in a different coat colour. To work backstitch, follow Fig 3, bringing the needle up at 1, down at 2, up at 3, and so on.

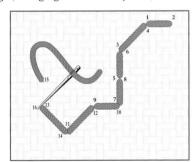

Fig 3 Backstitch

Cross Stitch

This can be worked singly or a number of half stitches can be sewn in a line and completed on the return journey.

To make a cross stitch over one block of Aida (Fig 4a), bring the needle up through the fabric at 1 and cross diagonally to 2. Push the needle through the hole and bring up at 3, crossing diagonally to finish at 4. To work the next stitch, come up through the bottom left corner of the first stitch and repeat the steps above.

To work a line of cross stitches, stitch the first part of the stitch as above and repeat these half cross stitches along the row. Complete the crosses on the way back (Fig 4b). Note: always finish the cross stitch with the top stitches lying in the same diagonal direction.

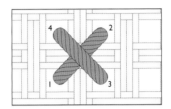
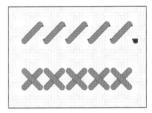

Fig 4a Single cross stitch
on Aida fabric

Fig 4b Cross stitch in two
journeys on Aida fabric

French Knot

French knots have been used as full stops in some of the alphabets. To work, follow Fig 5, bringing the needle and thread up through the fabric at the exact place where the knot is to be positioned. Wrap the thread twice around the needle, holding the thread firmly close to the needle, then twist the needle back through the fabric as close as possible to where it first emerged. Holding the knot down carefully, pull the thread through to the back leaving the knot on the surface, securing it with one small stitch on the back.

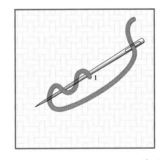

Fig 5 French knot

Three-quarter Cross Stitch

Three-quarter cross stitches give more detail to a design and can create the illusion of curves. They are shown by a triangle within a square on the charts (as in diagram below). To work, make a quarter stitch from the corner into the centre of the Aida square, piercing the fabric, and then work a half stitch across the other diagonal (Fig 6).

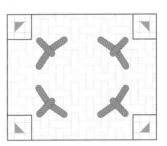

Fig 6 Three-quarter cross stitch

MAKING UP THE PROJECTS

The designs in this book are highly versatile and have been made up in many ways, with the techniques described here. See Suppliers for useful addresses.

MOUNTING WORK INTO READY-MADE ITEMS

Many of the designs in this book have been mounted into items specially made for displaying embroidery, including notebooks, coasters, rulers, pen holders, fridge magnets, key rings and name plates (see the notebook and framed picture right). Check the size of your planned stitching to ensure it will fit the item. Mount work following the manufacturer's instructions. Use paper or thin card to hide the back of any stitching that may be seen. It also helps to back the stitched design with iron-on interfacing (see below), to stiffen and prevent fabric fraying.

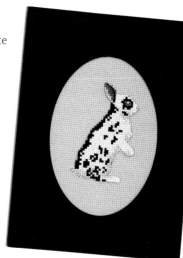

A notebook cover is the perfect place for a motif. This rabbit (page 69) is stitched on 14-count green Aida using two strands of stranded cotton (floss) for cross stitch and one for backstitch. The stitching is mounted into the notebook's aperture, which in this case is 14 x 10cm (5½ x 4in).

Stitch count: 47 x 31
Design size: 8.5 x 5.6cm
(3⅜ x 2¼in) on 14-count

There are many pre-finished items available to display your cross stitch – see Suppliers on page 104.

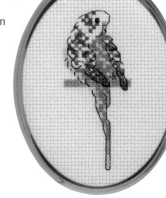

An elegant brass frame beautifully complements this blue budgerigar (page 80). The frame shown is 10 x 7.6cm (4 x 3in). The design is stitched on 14-count cream Aida using two strands of stranded cotton (floss) for cross stitch and one for backstitch, then mounted into the frame.

Stitch count: 44 x 19
Design size: 8 x 3.5cm
(3⅛ x 1⅜ in)

USING IRON-ON INTERFACING

Iron-on interfacing is used to back the stitched designs, to strengthen them and prevent fraying when cutting the fabric into shape. Using a heavyweight interfacing means designs can be shaped and stuck on to photo and picture frames or on to wood. Use a medium-weight interfacing to back embroidery patches which can then be applied to books and storage jars.

Cut a piece of interfacing a little larger than the finished design size (including any unworked fabric needed to fill an aperture or ready-made item). Set your iron to the manufacturer's recommended temperature, testing the heat first on waste fabric and interfacing to make sure that they will bond without scorching the design. Now place the stitching face down a towel and iron the interfacing on. After bonding trim off excess interfacing.

MAKING A TASSEL

It is easy to make your own tassel if you can't buy a ready-made one in the colour you need. Cut a rectangular piece of stiff card, about 1.25cm (½in) longer than the desired size of the tassel. Choose a thread colour or colours to match your project and wrap the thread around and around the card to the desired thickness. Slide the threads off the card, slip a length of thread through the top of the tassel loop and tie in a knot. Bind the top third of the tassel with another length of thread and then trim all the tassel ends to the same length.

MOUNTING WORK INTO A READY-MADE CARD

Any of the designs in this book would make lovely cards for someone who is mad about animals. Cards also make simple picture frames. The calendar on page 10 uses a card as a mount.

YOU WILL NEED

• a ready-made two-fold card • dressmaker's pins • double-sided adhesive tape •

1 Lay the card right side up on top of the design so the stitching is in the middle of the aperture. Place a pin at each corner and remove the card. Trim the fabric to within about 1.25cm (½in) so it will fit inside the card when it is made up.

2 On the wrong side of the card, stick double-sided tape around the aperture and peel off the backing strip. With the stitching right side up, place the card over the design, using the pins to guide it into position. Press down firmly around the aperture so the fabric is stuck securely to the card. Remove pins.

3 Place the card face down with the top of the design at the top. On the wrong side of the card, stick more double-sided tape around the edge of the middle section and peel off the backing tape. Fold in the left section to cover the back of the stitching and press down firmly. Fold in the right section to finish.

MAKING AN APERTURE CARD

You can make your own card mount if your design is too big for a ready-made card.

YOU WILL NEED

• sheet of plain paper • sharp scissors or craft knife • sheet of card in your chosen colour and texture • pencil and ruler •

1 Measure the width and height of the finished design and add 2cm (¾in) to each measurement. Draw a rectangle this size in the middle of the plain paper and cut out. Place this aperture over the design to check it fits.

2 Allowing a margin of 2cm (¾in), draw a rectangle around this aperture (the size of the finished mount). Place this paper template on to the wrong side of a piece of card, matching bottom edges. Draw around the outside edges of the template, move it along and draw another mount shape next to the first. Repeat once more so that you have a rectangle of three sections. Lightly score along the two lines separating the sections to help folding. Cut out the rectangle.

3 Place the template into the centre section and draw around the aperture. Carefully cut out the aperture. Trim a small amount from the left edge of the first section so it lies flat when folded over to the inside of the card. Fold in the left and right section along the scored lines. Mount your stitching following the instructions for a ready-made card left.

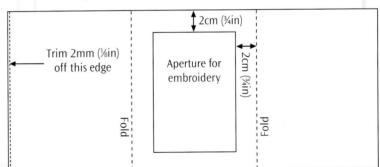

MAKING A DRAWSTRING BAG

The cross stitch designs in the book would be perfect to adorn a wide variety of bags. These instructions for the denim toy bag on page 11 could be easily adapted to suit other bag shapes. This finished bag is 35.5 x 40.5cm (14 x 16in) approximately.

YOU WILL NEED

• denim or furnishing fabric • piping cord or string •

1 Cut two pieces 38 x 48cm (15 x 19in) from your chosen fabric. Machine zigzag stitch around the edges to prevent fraying. On the wrong side, place two marks 9.5cm (3¾in) and 11.5cm (4½in) from the top on each long edge, to mark the drawstring channel.

2 Back the embroidery patch with iron-on interfacing (see opposite page). Turn in the edges and tack (baste). Pin and stitch into place on one fabric piece, making sure it is central.

3 Place the two pieces right sides together. Beginning at the top, sew the side seam, using a seam allowance of 1.5cm (⅝in), ending at the first mark. Beginning again at the second mark complete the seam – the gap is for the drawstring channel. Sew

the second side seam to match and then stitch across the bottom seam. Press seams open. Turn 6.5cm (2½in) over at the top and tack (baste) down. Make the channel by sewing two lines of stitching 3cm (1¼in) and 5cm (2in) from the top edge. Press, avoiding the patch, and turn through to the right side.

4 Thread a length of piping cord through the channel, starting and ending at one gap. Join the ends together with a knot. Thread another length through the other gap. Pull both loops to close the bag.

MAKING UP A FRAMED PICTURE

The samplers and many of the designs in this book make wonderful framed pictures and there are so many frames to choose from today.

YOU WILL NEED

• a frame to fit your embroidery • mount board • dressmaker's pins • thin wadding (batting) • double-sided adhesive tape •

1 Cut a piece of mount board to fit the frame aperture (draw around the glass that fits the frame, watching for any sharp edges). Using double-sided tape, stick a piece of wadding (batting) to the mount board and trim the wadding to the same size with a sharp craft knife. This will raise the surface slightly and show your stitching to better effect.

2 Lay the embroidery right side up on to the wadding, making sure the design is central and straight, matching a fabric thread along the edges. Push pins through at the four corners and along the edges to mark the position. Trim the fabric to leave 5cm (2in) all around.

3 Turn the embroidery and mount board over together. Stick double-sided tape around the edges of the board to a depth of 5cm (2in) and peel off the backing. Fold the excess fabric back,

pressing down firmly to stick the fabric to the board, adding more tape to neaten the corners. Remove pins and reassemble the frame with the embroidery in it. It is not necessary to use the glass; this often flattens the stitches when they are pushed against it.

MAKING A SIGN

Signs are so useful all around the house and office and there are plenty of alphabets and motifs to choose from, even unusual ones like gorgeous emerald tree boa on page 86.

YOU WILL NEED

• heavyweight iron-on interfacing • eyelet kit • twisted cord •

1 Trim the finished embroidery to size, allowing 1.5cm (⅝in) to turn to the wrong side. Neaten raw edges with machine zigzag stitch, turn under to the wrong side and press.

2 Cut two pieces of heavyweight iron-on interfacing the same size as the finished sign. Back the stitching with the two layers, one at a time, to make the sign rigid.

3 Using left-over stranded cotton (floss), top stitch around the sign, through all layers to secure the turned-back edges. Mark the positions for two eyelets on the top edge and use an eyelet kit as as instructed by the manufacturer. Cut a piece of hanging cord to size, thread it through the eyelets and secure with knots on the wrong side.

MAKING A WALL HANGING

A wall hanging, whether small or large, is wonderful for displaying cross stitch design, like the regal cat on page 47.

YOU WILL NEED

• cotton backing fabric • piping cord • wooden bell pull ends •

1 Stitch your design on to a piece of fabric with an extra 8cm (3in) at top and bottom (to fit around the wooden bell pull ends). When the stitching is finished, trim the fabric at each side to 2.5cm (1in), leaving the top and bottom untrimmed.

2 Cut a piece of backing fabric to the same size. Place the two pieces of fabric right sides together and stitch the side seams using a 1.5cm (⅝in) seam allowance. Turn through to the right side and press.

3 Fold the top and bottom edges around the wooden rods and pin into position. If need be, cut the wooden rods to size. Remove the rods and trim excess fabric. Neaten the raw edges with zigzag stitch and stitch the two channels for the rods. Insert the rods into the channels, and glue the knobs on to each end, inserting a hanging thread into the top ends.

MAKING UP THE WELCOME SAMPLER

This charming little sampler (page 5) shows how the simplest motifs can be combined to create something special.

◟ YOU WILL NEED ◝

• backing fabric • iron-on interfacing • a small quilt hanger •

1 On a piece of 14-count Aida fabric and using a tacking (basting) thread, mark an area 89 x 89 squares. Within this area, stitch the row of chickens at the top as they are on the chart (page 96), making sure they are centralized. Do the same for the row of ducks along the bottom edge.

2 On a piece of cream evenweave fabric, stitch 'Welcome' over two fabric threads, using the alphabet on page 65 and DMC colour 316. Trim the fabric to size and fray the edges. Stitch into place in the centre of the sampler.

3 Trim the fabric around the stitched design to within 2.5cm (1in) of the tacked (basted) line. Cut a piece of backing fabric the same size. With right sides facing and using a 1.5cm (⅝in) seam allowance, sew the two pieces together leaving the bottom seam open. Turn through to the right side, press and sew up the bottom seam.

4 Take another piece of cream Aida the same size as the sampler and back it with iron-on interfacing (see page 100). Cut two tabs 3.2 x 5.7cm (1¼ x 2¼in). Fold in half over the hanger and pin into position on the wrong side 2cm (¾in) from the side edges. Using DMC colour 316, topstitch around the sampler, working through all thicknesses of the tabs to secure them in place.

MAKING A BOOKMARK

A bookmark is easy to make and is a great gift for a friend. The one on page 79 is for a bird lover but many designs in this book would be equally suitable.

◟ YOU WILL NEED ◝

• dressmaker's pins • cotton backing fabric
• pencil and ruler • tassel (optional) •

1 Place pins to the right and left of the widest part of your embroidery, leaving a margin of 2.5cm (1in). Place a pin 4cm (1½in) above the top of the stitching. Decide on the length of your bookmark to fit around your design. Measure from the top pin down and place a pin. The pins mark the size of your bookmark with seam allowances. Trim the excess fabric.

2 Cut a piece of backing fabric the same size. With right sides together, tack (baste) along the sides. To make a pointed end, fold the bottom edge in half to find the middle and place a mark 1.5cm (⅝in) above this. Using a soft pencil and ruler, draw a line from each side to form a point. Don't make it too sharp or include any of the stitching. Using a seam allowance of 1.5cm (⅝in), stitch the side seams and the point. Trim the seam allowances and turn through to the right side, pushing the point out with the end of a pencil.

3 Press the bookmark and turn under the seam allowance along the top edges. Top stitch around the edges and across the top to close it. Stitch a tassel on to the point (see page 100 for making a tassel).

MAKING A HANGING CUSHION

The simplest design can be used to make a hanging cushion or sachet, like the one on page 67 – perfect for hanging on a hutch, kennel or cage, or your bedroom door!

◟ YOU WILL NEED ◝

• cotton backing fabric • polyester stuffing • piping cord •

1 Mark a square around the embroidery using tacking (basting) thread, making sure the design is in the centre. Cut to size and then cut backing fabric the same size. With right sides facing, stitch the two pieces together around three sides. Trim the seam allowance, turn through to the right side and press. Stuff the cushion with polyester stuffing and then sew the remaining seam closed.

2 Cut a piece of piping cord about 25cm (10in) long for a handle and sew into place on the top edge. Hand sew more piping cord around the edges of the cushion if desired.

SUPPLIERS

Contact individual manufacturers for your local stockist or find stockists and mail-order information on their website. If ringing from outside the UK use +44 and no (0).

UK

Coats Crafts UK

PO Box 22, Lingfield Estate, McMullen Road, Darlington, County Durham DL1 1YQ
tel: +44 (0) 1325 365457 (for stockists)
fax: +44 (0) 1325 338822

For Anchor stranded cotton (floss) and other embroidery supplies. Coats also supplies some Charles Craft products

Craft Creations Ltd

Ingersoll House, Delamare Road, Cheshunt, Hertfordshire, EN8 9HD
tel: 01992 781900
email: enquiries@craftcreations.com
www.craftcreations.com

For a wide range of craft items including ready-made cards, paper products and trimmings

DMC Creative World

Pullman Road, Wigston, Leicestershire LE18 2DY
tel: 0116 281 1040
fax: 0116 281 3592
www.dmc/cw.com

For stranded cotton (floss) and embroidery supplies

Framecraft Miniatures Ltd

Unit 3, Isis House, Lindon Road, Brownhills, West Midlands WS8 7BW
tel/fax (UK): 01543 360842
tel (international): 44 1543 453154
email: sales@framecraft.com
www.framecraft.com

For bell pull ends, brass frames, coasters, door plates, fridge magnets, key rings, notebooks, pen holders, rulers and many other pre-finished items with cross stitch inserts

Impress Cards and Craft Materials

Slough Farm, Westhall, Suffolk, IP19 8RN
tel: 01986 781422
email: sales@impresscards.co.uk
www.impresscards.com

For a wide range of craft materials including ready-made cards

Madeira Threads (UK) Ltd

PO Box 6, Thirsk, North Yorkshire YO7 3YX
tel: 01845 524880
email: info@madeira.co.uk
www.madeira.co.uk

For Madeira stranded cotton (floss) and other embroidery supplies

The Viking Loom

22 High Petergate, York YO1 7EH
tel: 01904 765599
www.vikingloom.co.uk

For bell pulls and linen bands

USA

The DMC Corporation

10 Port Kearney, South Kearney, NJ 070732
tel: 979 589 0606
www.dmc-usa.com

For DMC threads and fabrics and a wide range of needlework supplies

Gay Bowles Sales Inc

PO Box 1060, Janesville, WI 53547
tel: 608 754 9466
fax: 608 754 0665
email: millhill@inwave.com
www.millhill.com

For Mill Hill beads and a US source for Framecraft products

Yarn Tree Designs

PO Box 724, Ames, Iowa 500100724
tel: 1 800 247 3952
www.yarntree.com

For cross stitch supplies, card mounts and pre-finished items for embroidery

Zweigart/Joan Toggit Ltd

262 Old Brunswick Road, Suite E, Piscataway, NJ 08854-3756
tel: 732 562 8888
email: info@zweigart.com
www.zweigart.com

For a large selection of cross stitch fabrics and pre-finished items for embroidery

ACKNOWLEDGMENTS

I would like to thank DMC Creative World Ltd, UK, for their generosity in supplying all fabrics and threads used for the projects in this book and also Impress Cards for the card mounts.

ABOUT THE AUTHOR

Claire studied knitwear design at college before joining the design team at DMC, and finally going freelance. Claire's work has appeared in several magazines, including *Cross Stitch Magic*. Her designs also feature in *Cross Stitch Greetings Cards*, *Cross Stitch Alphabets*, *Cross Stitch Angels* and *Cross Stitch Fairies*. Her first solo book for David & Charles, *Cross Stitch Card Collection*, was followed by *The Knitter's Bible*, published in 2004. Claire lives in the Tamar Valley, Cornwall, UK.

INDEX